Island of Bones

AMERICAN LIVES

Series editor

Tobias Wolff

Island of Bones

Essays

JOY CASTRO

University of Nebraska Press · Lincoln and London

Library of Congress
Cataloging-in-Publication Data

Castro, Joy.
Island of bones: essays / Joy Castro.
p. cm. — (American lives)
Includes bibliographical references.
ISBN 978-0-8032-7142-5 (pbk.: alk. paper)
1. Castro, Joy—Family. 2. Castro, Joy—Child-
hood and youth. 3. English teachers—United
States—Biography. 4. Jehovah's Witnesses—
Biography. 5. Abused children—United
States—Biography. 6. Children of divorced
parents—United States—Biography. I. Title.
PE64.C37A3 2012 420'92—dc23
[B]
2012003416

Set in Garamond Premier Pro by Kim Essman.
Designed by A. Shahan.

For Virginia, Rosie, and Dolores

Pero es difícil differentiating between
lo heredado, lo adquirido, lo impuesto.

—GLORIA ANZALDÚA,
Borderlands/La Frontera: The New Mestiza

Contents

1   Island of Bones

11   What My Mother Told Me
When I Found Her

13   Clips of My Father's House

17   Turn of Faith

20   Getting Lost

23   In Theory

27   Farm Use

36   Hip Joints

47   No *Más* Monkey

50   Edging

54   Fitting

59   The Athens of the Midwest

68 You Can Avoid the Mistakes I Made

70 An Angle of Vision

80 Grip

82 Getting "Grip"

89 Hungry

93 On Becoming Educated

102 Vesper Adest

106 "¿Quién es ese Jimmy Choo?":
     A Latina Mother Comes of Age

123 GRATITUDE

125 SOURCE ACKNOWLEDGMENTS

127 NOTES

131 BIBLIOGRAPHY

Island of Bones

HOME

The anthologies don't mention us. When I teach Latino studies, I have to take supplemental materials into class so that students know Cubans existed here in the United States before 1959.

In the public narrative of Cuban immigration, the narrative we most often hear and read, we're told that, fleeing Castro's revolution, the very *"first* wave of Cubans, approximately 250,000, arrived from 1959 to 1964"—emphasis mine—as Guillermo Grenier writes in his study of Cuban American exile ideology. Two other major cohorts swiftly followed—all of them middle and upper class, highly educated, and professional—before the poorer, less skilled Marielitos arrived in 1980. According to this narrative, moreover, Cuban Americans lean right: they vote Republican, since ousting Castro's regime is the primary factor that motivates their politics and also since they're well-to-do and want to protect the wealth they brought with them or earned, once on Floridian soil, through their industry and thrift.

But this narrative erases an earlier succession of small waves of nineteenth-century Cuban immigrants—not political exiles, but people who came to the United States in search of work, like economic immigrants who come from Mexico and Central and South America today. By the 1890s, half the population of Key West—Cayo Hueso, the isle of bones—was Cuban, including *mi familia*, who had begun emigrating there from Cuba in the 1870s. Over the decades before Fidel Castro came to power, the Rolo and then the Castro family ran the Spanish-language printing press on the island. My family belonged to a working-class community of skilled and unskilled laborers, and its ties to Cuba were strong. National Airlines, for which my father would eventually work as a skycap, ticket agent, and then manager, ran flights to Havana from 1946 to 1961. Before Castro's revolution, my grandparents went back regularly to reconnect with relatives.

But Cayo Hueso is a small island, its Cuban history a small history that has mostly been erased from our national memory by the dramatic convulsions of the revolution, the Bay of Pigs, the Cuban Missile Crisis, little Elián and Janet Reno. Key West's own status in the public imagination, like the status of most Caribbean islands, is simply that of resort playground.

MONEY

Between 1959 and 1979, most of the Cubans who came to Florida were well-to-do middle- and upper-class people frustrated with the communist takeover, and they were welcomed here as good capitalists. Within their cultural productions here in the United States since then, Cuba shimmers like a lost Eden of servants, mansions, pleasure, and beauty. It's a vision that wealth-loving Americans have been all too happy to endorse. Carlos Eire's memoir *Waiting for Snow in Havana*, for example, which won the National Book Award, opens with his family members referring to themselves as French royalty while they frolic among their heirloom furniture and porcelain, unaware of the impending revolution. Mary Urrutia Randelman's cookbook *Memories of a Cuban Kitchen* is laced with photos of her family's fifteen-hundred-acre tobacco plantation, their fourteen-thousand-acre cattle ranch (granted by the king of Spain), members of her family at the Havana Yacht Club, and her laughing parents, sailing off Varadero Beach. In her detective novels, Carolina Garcia-Aguilera deploys the common cultural stereotype of the Miami Cuban who dunks buttered Cuban toast in his coffee, bemoaning his exile twenty years after the fact, and whose yacht is pointed toward Havana, ready to go as soon as the radio proclaims good news. In her recent autobiographical one-woman play *Rum & Coke*, Carmen Peláez waxes nostalgic about her family's lost wealth and privilege. I sat in the audience wanting to puke, wondering, *Is this the only story Cubans know how to tell? I can't connect with these people.*

Neither can my aunt, my only relative (out of dozens) who still remains on the island. As a librarian at Key West High, she can barely afford to live there, now that it's been chopped into resorts for the wealthy. All of our other relatives have moved north.

When I was in grad school in Texas, I asked her why she didn't move to Miami.

"Ugh," she said. "Too many Cubans."

At the time, full of youthful hubris and new paradigms from ethnic studies, I diagnosed her with a sad case of internalized racism. Later I learned that, like my father did, and like I do, she leans left politically and that "Cubans," to her, signifies the right-wing Cubans who dominate the news, the post-1959 Cubans—angry, well-to-do, horn honking, and proud of their passion—and not the Key West Cubans she grew up with, not her family and friends. The dominant media coverage has erased her own story—even for her.

My family members are a little socialist, honestly, but not in a very political kind of way. We're mostly poor people, workers, cleaners of other people's houses, grocery checkers, cops. *Ranchos* and servants don't really do it for us. We'd like economic justice, yeah, but we don't quite know what to do about it; most of us aren't exactly reading Marx and Engels on the weekend. We're just kind of skeptical of the capitalist metanarrative, the way most poor, working-class, and lower-middle-class workers—or people who grew up that way—are.

We're sure not waxing nostalgic for a Cuba where we were only poorer, where none of my great-aunts bought dresses at El Encanto.

We weren't part of El Movimiento. We lack a political identity. "I'm just a Conch," says my aunt, referring to the term for Key West natives.

With property values on the island the way they are, there are almost no Conchs left.

NOSTALGIA

A conch shell sits on my *altár*. My dad gave it to me. (I never called him Apá; he made us use English at home—another source of Latino identity, busted.) He used to dive for conchs as a boy. He used to shimmy up coconut palms and throw the coconuts down. When we were children, he'd crack them open and let us drink the sweet, thin milk.

He committed suicide in 2002. I still wonder what part loneliness played. For decades he pursued the American Dream, moving wherever the job required, working to assimilate, laughing off the way white people compared him to Ricky Ricardo: Miami, London, West Virginia, a man with only a high school education trying to play in the white-collar world with just his silver tongue and smarts. It worked for a while, until his age caught up with him and suddenly every entry-level applicant had a degree, and he watched his career spiral away as he sank from a small-time airline executive to a collection agent to a census taker, walking door to door in rural West Virginia, watching out for dogs.

His suicide ruptures the myth. Latinos, history tells us, don't kill themselves. They nobly sacrifice and organize like Chávez or take up arms like Tijerina. They're heroes, like Pancho Villa and Emiliano Zapata. Call them Joaquín. They labor and sacrifice; they boss their wives and children; they *endure* for the sake of *familia*, for *dignidad*. They do not go gentle into that good night.

But my dad did. No macho, he washed dishes and fried eggs and died alone in his Chevy.

Tidy, my stepmother said. The bullet hole was barely noticeable. He died with his eyes closed. He looked sad, she said, as if he'd been sleeping and was having a sad, sad dream.

GOD

Latinos are Catholic, or so goes the narrative, and Latinas are particularly devout. Our hair is choked with the smoke of copal and candles, our homes plastered with images of saints and *la Virgen* and the sacred heart of Jesus.

But my *abuela* in Key West, with her seventh-grade education and four kids and exhaustion (plus a slew of the neighbors' children to watch for extra money), opened her door on Elizabeth Street one day to a Jehovah's Witness, and boy, didn't it all sound good: paradise on Earth, starting any minute now (as soon as Jehovah wipes out the wicked—and you *know* Aunt Poni's gonna get it, the way she carries on), and everybody getting a big, nice house with a landscaped lawn like in the pictures in *The Watchtower*, and all your kids behaving for once, and no racism, and everybody with enough to eat and new clothes and equal in the eyes of the Lord. Just like that, she threw off generations of Catholicism and orishas and dragged her kids out of Mass and straight to the Kingdom Hall, and that's how they grew up. My aunt Lettie even married an elder. My dad, who'd been an altar boy, gave talks from the stage about Jehovah, and when he married a pretty National Airlines stewardess, they held the ceremony in the Key West Kingdom Hall.

My brother and I grew up not with saints and candles, not with Oshun and Yemaya, but with a squeaky-clean Jesus, dreaming of the tigers we'd have for pets (as soon as Armageddon hurried up and got here) and preaching door to door.

Island of Bones 5

I left the Witnesses at fifteen. As an adult, I tried the Catholic Church, but higher education had already excised my tolerance for dogma, so I settled, like many academics, into a secular agnosticism, spiritual-but-not-religious. I might chant, meditate, and pray—but not *to* anyone. Why I felt the need for a rosary, which dangles over my desk, or why I mutter the Hail Mary when planes take off is anyone's guess.

On the wall by my desk brood images of the Virgin: la Virgen de Guadalupe, Cuba's Virgen de la Caridad del Cobre, and Spain's black Virgin of Montserrat. But they weren't the ones I prayed to growing up.

LOOKS

I have brown hair, brown eyes, and light skin. Growing up, it was always, "Ay, qué linda," and, "You look just like your father." My aunts are light skinned, too. *Mi prima* Jeri has blue eyes, and when she gets highlights, the pale streaks look natural. In Miami, where people know that Cubans span the color wheel from black to blond, it's not an issue.

But heritage doesn't always translate visually. Here in Nebraska, I was waiting outside the yoga studio the other day. A guy from my class was also waiting: a Chicano. He asked how things were going.

I told him how happy I was with the Latino studies class I'm teaching this semester, and he drew back in surprise.

"No disrespect," he said, "but what qualifies *you* to teach Latino studies?"

Other than a PhD? I wondered. But I explained my background.

"Oh. Oh, sorry. I know some Cubans," he said, "and you don't look Cuban."

Then I pointed out that if he takes Latino studies seriously as an intellectual discipline, identity shouldn't be a prerequisite. No one asks a Shakespeare scholar if he or she is a British male playwright from the sixteenth century. He laughed and conceded the point.

I often forget about my appearance, but I know that to people like my yoga friend I don't look Latina, and my spoken English has only the bland, mongrelized sound of frequent moves among disparate places—Florida, England, West Virginia, Texas, the Midwest—so there's no accent to indicate ethnicity. With my *latinidad* so muted, I sometimes wonder if I should work harder at staging it, in order to signal both my solidarity *con otras* Latinas and my difference from the mainstream. But what would that entail? Big silver hoops in my ears? Red lipstick? Snug skirts and a salsa sway? The polka-dotted halter dresses and head wraps that one visually ambiguous *cubana* friend chooses to wear? But I resent all the jungle exoticism that's foisted on Latinas, from J. Lo on down, so why would I invoke it? For Latinas, performing our gendered ethnic identity always seems to include the notion of heat, spice, a tasty sensuality offered up for consumption.

As a writer, I've always felt like a thinking subject. As a feminist, I've never longed to be an object. The watcher, not the watched. Why should I go around declaring my ethnic identity all the time, as if the whole world were a customs agent, inspecting me?

BLOOD

But it's more complicated than that, even, because when I tell the guy at yoga class, "Oh, my family's Cuban," the fact is, I'm passing.

In 1967, when the attorney told my infertile parents (who paid a thousand dollars for the legal right to take me home) that I was a Latina baby, they believed him. Growing up, so did I. Given that the adoption took place in Miami, we all presumed I was probably *cubana*, or maybe *dominicana* or *colombiana*. To fill in the gaps that my closed adoption left, I invented elaborate scenarios: my Catholic schoolgirl mother, unable to destroy her child of passion, sang like Maria in *West Side Story* to my devoted but star-crossed sire, pleading down in the street below like some *vato* Romeo. Sobbing her farewells in Spanish, she relinquished me reluctantly to the nuns.

I was sure that one day I would find her, meet her. To prepare, I read U.S. Latina literature—from all cultures, just to be sure: Sandra Cisneros, Julia Alvarez, Esmeralda Santiago, Isabel Allende, Judith Ortiz Cofer, Lorna Dee Cervantes, Marjorie Agosín. *Each one of these stories*, I would think, *could be my mother's.* For each, I opened a space in my heart.

In this way, my identity crystallized during adolescence and young adulthood in a kind of pan-Latina formation that was and remains deeply personal, deeply felt.

As any adoptee can tell you, meeting one's birthmother is strange and intense for all sorts of reasons. When I was twenty-six, I met mine, a nice Midwestern lady of Irish, French, and Swedish descent. (Like many Americans, she also claims Cherokee heritage, and it seems plausible, since most of her relatives live in Oklahoma and tell the same story about an ancestor walking the Trail of Tears. My maternal grandmother was a wasp-waisted girl with dark hair and big dark eyes.) My birthmother had taken buses to Miami for the pregnancy and birth, so no one in her hometown of Rockford, Illinois, would know.

I wasn't Latina at all.

In one sudden yank of the rug, I felt my family and identity severed from me. I didn't know where to stand. I didn't want anyone to accuse me of being a faker, a trespasser, a poser, a claimer of things not mine.

For about ten years, I claimed nothing.

NOW

At forty-three, when I say I'm Latina, it's a shortcut. It's true, and it gets you quickly to what I want you to know, but it's a falsification, too, a simplification, a smoothing over of layers of complication, deconstruction, loss, of chronic self-interrogation, multiple erasures, and years of painful reconstruction. A delicate, tentative claim I stake.

Ethnicity is complicated, and everyone has an opinion. During my midthirties, it was an African American friend who kept prodding me, shaking her head. "You're not white," she kept saying. "I don't know what you are, but you sure aren't white."

Later, I told a half-Latina, half-white friend about it. "What's wrong with white?" she snapped. "I hate that attitude."

Sometimes I just wanted to disappear.

Today I write from a small place, a complicated island with a history that's almost been lost. I write from a place of clear lip balm and jeans, of a PhD but no love for academia, of no talent in the kitchen (and thus no *Like Water for Chocolate* imitations, no homages to my grandmother's perfect garlic roast pork). I write from a keen and pissed-off class awareness and the streaming juice of very few mangoes.

Don't get me wrong: I like mangoes just fine, and key limes, and avocadoes straight from the tree, *verdad*, but I write with a prickly awareness of the easy appetite among mainstream readers for a romanticized, exoticized version of *latinidad*—a simplified, delicious version I could purvey, a version that would pleasure and sell.

But I don't want to help readers "eat the other," in the words of bell hooks. I don't want to teach you how to dance salsa or spoon you my grandmother's flan—and I sure as hell don't want to perform my sexual badness and write about big, dark nipples and violence for the upper-middle-class, educated, white people who read the *New Yorker* and listen to NPR. Providing a delectable frisson of dark, sexy danger is not my literary goal.

Academic Latino studies and ethnic studies programs have done much to articulate—even privilege—the experience and idea of border crossing. Hybridity's hip, and we've all been schooled to admire the supple complexities of liminality. Yet borders still abound, and the risk of crossing them is the same risk it has always been: invisibility, erasure, obliteration. There's solidarity in numbers; there's psychic safety in fitting the stereotypes. Readers and publishers know where to slot you, and when national book distribution boils down, as it does, to thirty seconds of negotiation between your publisher's marketing rep and the Barnes & Noble guy with his laptop open, checking sales figures of past books like yours, it helps if you're simple to sum up.

What happens when a Latina not only doesn't look the part but also doesn't write the part? What happens to Latina writers who cross not only boundaries of nation and culture in their lives but also borders of genre and subject matter in their work? When the content and style of Latina literary productions confound market expectations and publishers' readymade packaging plans, what happens to those manuscripts? What about experimental work that editors believe will baffle Latino *y* Latina book buyers, whom they believe to be less educated and thus less capable of reading complicated work? *Híjole.*

For me, all the myths have come undone. I don't fit. I don't fit, and that's okay, and that's where I write from: that jagged, smashed place of edges and fragments and grief, of feeling lost, of perilous freedom. I extract small fragile bones from the sand, dust them off with my brush, and build strange, urgent new structures, knowing too well how small my island is, how vast and rising the sea.

What My Mother Told Me
When I Found Her

I was alone in Miami then, staying with a girlfriend who'd gotten mar-
ried. Her husband didn't want me there, didn't know me, claimed I was
a bad influence on the children. At night, they'd argue.

"It won't be much longer," my friend would say. "October."

The abortion hadn't worked. Lenny had driven me to the industrial
park in Peoria. I gave the man our two hundred dollars. He didn't look
like a doctor. He took me to a room further back in the warehouse while
Lenny waited on a folding chair. He told me to close my eyes and relax.
He put things in me and took them out, played around down there.
Then he told me to go home. It hadn't seemed so bad. Lenny drove to
Chinatown, and we ate dinner. I sat with my head on his shoulder all
the way home. He'd let me, now. He was affectionate again, now that
I'd done it.

But nothing happened. It was still in there, and we had no more
money. My mother, the only other person in Rockford who knew, said
my father would kill me if he found out. He'd beaten me before. I'd seen
him beat my brothers. I left the farm alone.

I took buses to Miami and found a job in a hospital, planning nutritious meals for the Seventh-Day Adventists. I bought a ring to wear so people wouldn't ask questions. This was 1967, you understand. Sometimes even married women had to leave their jobs when they started to show.

My friend wanted to adopt the baby, but she slapped her kids. I didn't want that. She drank, too. I'd wake up early with the children and give them breakfast while she slept it off.

I wandered the hot streets. Sometimes I'd sit in playgrounds and watch the mothers with their children. I folded my left hand over my right so my ring would show and I could sit there without embarrassment. The women were nice. It was like a club. They'd chat with me on the benches, and I'd say how far along I was and lie about my husband and our little bungalow in Hialeah and how we hoped you'd love the beach as much as we did.

I used to wait for the city bus at a shopping center, and sometimes I'd walk through the stores for the shade and large cooling fans, the soothing whir they made. Once I stopped in a long aisle like a tunnel, and rising on both sides around me, extending on metal arms from the pegboard, were baby clothes: yellow chenille cardigans, no bigger than my outstretched hand, with happy ducks sewn on; the soft film of receiving blankets, pink and blue; tiny white dresses with eyelet ruffles; soft small socks like pockets for a thumb, their cuffs rimmed in lace. I knew you'd be a girl. Against the thin skin of my belly I could feel you moving as I ran my hands across those fine small things. Delicate, they were so delicate, the crocheted booties, the little colored tights, so small and soft and bright in the dim high tunnel of the aisle, so light and flimsy. I stood there, stroking for what seemed like the longest time, feeling your strange push inside me and their softness collapsing against my fingers. I couldn't leave, couldn't move, couldn't imagine the man and woman who would buy these things for you.

"Ma'am," the clerk said, suddenly beside me, clearing his throat, "do you need some help?"

Clips of My Father's House

Nanny hated my lazy ways.

"Sweep," she would say, handing me a broom and pointing to the long driveway rolled flat as a bedsheet from Elizabeth Street to the print shop. I would stand in the sun, my hands gripped around the wood, pushing the thin silt side to side.

"I don't know how to sweep," I'd wail when she'd come out to chide me. It was true. My mother had grown up in Illinois, in a world where the mothers cleaned and the children played: she left me to my devices. But Nanny had quit school in seventh grade to help take care of her little brothers and sisters: idle girls made her nervous.

"Crazy. Crazy like your father, but with the books. Always your face in a book. *Mira*," she would say, slapping a wet sponge into my hand. Look. "Wipe."

When her big sister died, she married the widower and kept his house and raised his child and gave him four more. She washed their clothes and gave them baths and woke at five to start cooking the hot lunches for the men who'd come in sweaty from the print shop at noon to sit at the long table in the kitchen. Black beans and saffron rice and garlic pork and applesauce, *papas rellenos* and *tamales*, and for dessert key lime pie and sliced mangoes from the yard.

My aunts could clean a house and cook a meal by the time they were ten, and even my father, Nanny's only son—and her favorite, my aunts said, for no good reason but that he was a damn boy—even he could clean a bathroom, wash dishes, fry an egg to change your life. My aunt Linda got so good at cleaning houses that when she grew up she did it for a living in Miami, and the people liked her work so much, fast and quiet and leaving no dust, they gave her things: toys that still worked, kitchen appliances, suits that were old but still very nice, good quality even if not so stylish.

I was the oldest child of the only son, the one who got away, the one who made his parents proud and broke their hearts by leaving. He changed his name from Libano to Lee and said goodbye, and we lived in a place with rain and cold weather in the world he'd needed to see. But every summer we flew eight hours and drove down the linked bridges to stay, sleeping in rooms painted pale green, pale lilac, my parents in one, the girl cousins allowed to sleep over with me in the other. Whispering, giggling, we'd fall asleep to the whir of electric fans propped in each window. Each window had its screen, but nothing could stop the red bumps from rising on our legs in the morning. On our backs, we would count them, on our backs with our legs straight up, the sheets kicked aside in a tangle, and the one with the most was the sweetest.

Those rooms were kept darkened all day, their clattery green blinds shut tight. We couldn't play there—even our Barbies had to come outside under the mango trees to play in the rot of damp leaves.

We would run races down the driveway, screaming, our rubber sandals spanking the bright cement, our hands smacking the print shop wall in triumph. Outside, we never had to be quiet.

Inside, Nanny and the aunts heard everything and wanted you to shut up. Or get out of the house.

So we'd sit on the cool tile of the front porch, taking turns two at a time on the swing. We'd walk down to the candy store, jumping over the great banyan roots that split the sidewalk, and spend all our money, or beg a grown-up to take us fishing off the docks. Back at the house, we'd sit on the steps that ran up the outside of the house to where the renters lived. We'd sit by the open window and listen to the grown-ups, braiding each other's hair. Lulled by the sunshine and Susie's quick fingers against my neck, I let my mind go soft, let my self blur, indistinguishable from my cousins.

The driveway's a swimming pool now. Two interior decorators from Miami bought the house when Papi died and Nanny moved to the retirement apartments. I visited her there once on spring break. She kept showing me how easy everything was to take care of, how small the rooms were, how quick to vacuum. She and the old ladies sat around talking about how they wanted their funerals to be.

The print shop is a guest cabana.

When my father was a boy, he was crazy for the movies. He wanted to be in the movies, to make movies, to write movies. Just to be around the movies. Every Saturday he went to the Strand or the San Carlos, sitting through two or three showings in a row. When he was twelve, he owned little reels you could buy at the camera store—Laurel and Hardy, Buster Keaton—and he would show them on the celadon wall of the print shop on Sundays, a nickel an hour to the neighborhood kids. He was going to be directing the movies, he told them, and starring in them, too, when he felt like it.

But there wasn't money for film school, for college, for anything: he started out driving a truck instead.

Four minutes of home movie still exist, filmed when he was seventeen, the year before he left home. My father sits me down in his living room, a thousand miles away. West Virginia. It's snowing.

"Okay, watch now," he says. The tape starts rolling. "*Mira, mira,*" he says, tapping my arm when the focus clears. The colors are faded. Uncle Mario is setting type, screwing the letters into the rectangular frame. He pulls a lever; it slaps into place. Papi slices what looks like a machete through reams of fresh paper. My father the teenager stacks neat dozens of notepads and wraps them in tan parcel wrap. His hair is slicked down, black, shining. His khakis are belted. His eyes are young and brown.

No one looks at the camera, which makes it all seem very serious: a documentary of printing in the 1950s in Key West. "I told them to do that," my father says eagerly. "I kept telling them not to look up at me."

No one does.

Turn of Faith

Adopted at birth by a family of Jehovah's Witnesses, I was required from an early age to behave as much like an adult as possible.

At five, I sat onstage in the Kingdom Hall in Surrey, England, where my father's job had taken us. Nervously pushing my memorized lines into the microphone, I faced my mother, who was seated across from me. We were demonstrating for the congregation exactly how a Bible study with a worldly person, a non-Witness, should go.

I had played the householder before—the person who answered the door. That was easy; you just asked questions that showed you didn't know the Truth. Portraying the Witness was harder: you had to produce the right Bible verse to counter any objection the householder might raise.

But we had written our parts on index cards and rehearsed repeatedly at home. I was well dressed and shining clean. I recited my lines flawlessly and gave looks of concern at the right times. Finally, the householder agreed with everything I had said: her way of life was wicked, and the Bible clearly proved that the Witnesses were the only true Christians who would be saved at Armageddon. Her facial expression looked earnest and grateful. Then she smiled, becoming my mother again. When everyone clapped, she glowed with pride. At last I could go out in service.

From then on, I knocked on the doors of strangers each week with a memorized script that urged them to repent. I didn't play with worldly children. I didn't have birthday parties or Christmas mornings. What I did was pray a lot. I knew the books of the Bible in order, by heart, and could recite various verses. My loneliness was nourished by rich, beautiful fantasies of eternal life in a paradise of peace, justice, racial harmony, and environmental purity, a recompense for the rigor and social isolation of our lives.

This bliss wasn't a future we had to work for. Witnesses wouldn't vote, didn't involve themselves in worldly matters, weren't activists. Jehovah would do it all for us, destroying everyone else and restoring the earth to harmony. All we had to do was wait and obey.

Shortly after our return to the States, my father was disfellow-shipped for being an unrepentant smoker—smoking violated God's temple, the body, much like fornication and drunkenness. Three times a week in the Kingdom Hall in Miami, my brother and I strove to sit perfectly still in our chairs. Our mother carried a wooden spoon in her purse and was quick to take us outside for beatings if we fidgeted.

When I was ten in West Virginia, my parents' marriage dissolved, and both quickly remarried. My mother's second husband had served at Bethel, the Watchtower's headquarters in Brooklyn. The Witnesses' doctrines, based on Paul's letters in the New Testament, gave him complete control as the new head of the household; my mother's role was to submit. My stepfather happened to be the kind of person who took advantage of this authority, physically abusing us, raping my mother, sexually abusing me, and forcing my brother and me to shun our father completely. Though the elders at our Kingdom Hall knew about the physical violence, they merely encouraged my mother toward greater wifely submission.

At fourteen, I ran away to live with my father. My brother joined us a tumultuous six months later. The two of us continued to attend the Kingdom Hall and preach door to door; the Witnesses had been our only community. Leaving was a gradual process that took months of questioning. At fifteen, I decided that I could no longer be part of a religion that condoned inequality, much less violence.

After my stepfather finally went to prison for molesting a nine-year-old girl, my mother divorced him, moved out of state, and married another Witness. I feel for her. A smart, capable woman, she subjugated her will and judgment, as the Witnesses teach, to her husband's. If she damaged my brother and me or failed to protect us, she did so out of fear and belief. She wanted to save us from certain destruction at Armageddon, from a corrupt and dirty world. She wanted nothing less for us than paradise.

I love my mother, but I also love my "worldly" life, the multitude of ideas I was once forbidden to entertain, the rich friendships and the joyous love of my family. Our rare correspondence skates over the surface of our strained détente. By choosing to live in the world she scorned—to teach at a university, to spare the rod entirely, to believe in the goodness of all kinds of people—I have, in her eyes, turned my back not only on Jehovah but also on her.

When Jehovah's Witnesses come to my door now, I know discussion is futile; they have a carefully planned response for any objection. Finally, I say, "I'm an apostate," and their eyes widen at the word: someone who has willfully rejected Jehovah, far worse than a worldly person, who is simply ignorant of the Truth. A threat to the faith of others, an apostate deserves to be shunned, as we were forced to shun our disfellowshipped father.

The Witnesses back away from my door.

Getting Lost

Getting lost was a gift my father gave me. Every Saturday morning when I was a little girl, we would drive off for our weekly "explore" through the countryside of England, where our family had moved for his job. At each asphalt crossroads he'd pause and turn to me, and—based on the fat pony to the right or an alluring dip in the road to the left—I'd choose our route. He'd twirl the wheel, and off we'd go until the next intersection, where I'd get to choose again.

When the road ran straight and there were no cars in sight, he'd ask, "Where do you want to go?"

"Windsor Castle," I'd reply, knowing what was coming. Twisting the wheel, he'd swerve us around the empty road as I shrieked, my terror and delight complete.

We'd get ourselves happily lost, finding a pub when hungry, stopping to feed ducks, tease cows, or clamber over stone ruins. We would chatter and wander together after the long week of work and school, of repeated nights when he'd arrive home late, after I was already asleep, from his job at London Heathrow Airport.

Saturday mornings were deliciously agenda-free. We were aimless, and the wondrous world beckoned. I loved the mystery of getting lost, the thrill of sudden swerves, and the heady power of telling my father what to do.

For me, writing's like that: an opportunity to get lost, to amble, to poke through ruins, to scare myself—but within a frame of faith, a faith that's like a buoy, both anchored and floating at once. Spill out whatever you want; the page will hold you up.

Writing provides a way to make sense, in language, of the puzzling, wild, beautiful moments our lives keep delivering to us: *Here*, whispers Life. *Figure this one out.* Offering us psychic space, privacy, and slowness in a rushed and noisy world, writing gives us the chance to tell our secrets, voice our own perceptions. It's the psychological equivalent of having the house to yourself for a whole evening and playing whatever music you want, with no one to see you dance around. As Sandra Cisneros wrote of her character's desire for a literal house in *The House on Mango Street*, "Only a house quiet as snow, a space for myself to go, clean as paper before the poem."

Writing can be a home. In our daily lives, we're besieged by the voices of other people: bosses, coworkers, politicians, TV—even the people we love. Writing lets us hear our own voices at length, in peace. It gives us the chance to follow the thread of our own thought to the center of the maze—and to slay or befriend whatever monsters lurk there.

There comes a time for many writers when writing for the self is not enough, when we hunger for feedback or suggestions. In that half-shy, half-hopeful stage, it helps to have someone who might know how to help shape this wild thing that's surged into your notebook.

That's my day job. As a literature and creative writing teacher, I've seen a lot of stories come and go. In nonfiction classes I've learned from my students about unmanned drones in Pakistan, cattle birthing in Nebraska, civil war in Sri Lanka, and the origins of Earl Grey tea. I've gotten lost in the stories of others, which are inevitably fascinating and humbling, and which have widened my world. In writing classes, students learn to care not only for each other's work, which they faithfully read and critique, but also for each other. They become communities of art-makers, dedicated to helping texts become clearer, tighter, more precise and moving. Some groups enjoy this so much that they keep meeting even after we've officially ended. But most are temporary, drawn together for a few fragile, valuable months.

Books about writing abound, and I have my favorites, but many craft books seem to want to classify and tame what has always felt, to me, essentially wild. Mysterious. Urgent, magical, free. Boringly, such books break writing's alchemy down into its safe constituent parts, when I'd rather just see what ignites.

But the best writing books encourage us, and we need encouragement. Getting lost is a risk. Most arenas of life—and most well-meaning people in our lives—urge us onto safe, pre-trodden paths. Choosing instead to take that risk, day after day, year after year—when the world, in most cases, hardly clamors for the products of our pens—demands quiet courage and a particular persistence. Continuing to write requires the renewal of a childlike curiosity—where might this road lead?—in the face of daily labors that can crush such wonder away.

Persisting in the writer's life takes a certain kind of faith, in the sense that people mean when they talk about faith in marriage: faith that within a chosen structure, the people involved will continue changing and freshening and being alive and will notice and welcome those changes in each other—that they will not turn off, shut down, go through the motions. Fidelity. The notebook may look like the same notebook, year after year; one's beloved may look only a very little changed. But inside, he or she is different, someone new.

Inside, you are different, too: never the same river twice. And this is the long exploration—the faithful, wondering marriage to the self—that writing permits and invites.

So do it. Let yourself get lost.

In Theory

A creosote bush is born into aridity, welcomed into the desert by winds and lack and thirst. But the creosote is also a blessed creature, plain and foul-tasting; the desert animals leave it to its own devices.

Sprouting from a central trunk, the creosote's supple branches are dark from the moment they emerge, black beneath the skin, charred in the womb of the plant. Leaves the size of fingernails unfurl, eschewing the luxury of exposure.

The creosote grows a little each year, but with a hollowness at the center. An empty space: its trunks grow up from the sand in a small ring. For the second decade, the third even, the branches may overlap, obscuring the empty center, but after a very few years more, two people could stand comfortably inside the ring, two people who might be only acquaintances. Or lovers so deeply wed they did not need to touch with their bodies. Strangers could stand there with some awkwardness, perhaps.

A creosote bush grows in increasing concentric circles, a circle widening year by year in the infallible memory of itself. One ring after another dies, loosening and opening: more space. More light dazzles the empty sand within.

Theoretically, a small party could transpire within a creosote bush of a certain age. Several people could lean against sofas, holding mixed drinks. Music could play, and a host and hostess could link arms in the kitchen. A woman could drink too much cognac and begin to talk to her best friend's husband. She could lean toward him, inclining like a tautened bow. Her hand could laugh across his cheek, grazing away crumbs that were not there. Her eyes could suddenly hold the promise of all he wept for as a child. His wife could be talking in the kitchen, not noticing the grazing fingers, the figures bending toward one another so that he begins to smell the woman, his wife's best friend, so that he begins to smell her perfume and the skin beneath the perfume and the promise in the skin. The hour could grow late, the guests could begin to leave. The headiness of the cognac could start to fade, the man could think of his children. A creosote bush is large enough to contain these things.

There is nothing naive about a creosote bush. Some may, in fact, be the oldest living creatures on Earth. They have seen the hippopotamus, the tapir, two kinds of camel, three species of Eohippus, and the ancestor of the modern bison dwell and disappear in North America. They have watched the climate change with the lessening rainfall. They have thirsted as their lusher companions departed. There is little that a creosote bush has not seen.

In theory, a girl could lie on the ground next to a hotel bed within such a bush. Her brother could lie at the foot of the bed. The woman in the bed could reach down to take her daughter's hand, and the man in the bed could begin to mutter, the woman to reply. The fingers of the woman could begin to tighten around the fingers of her daughter. The little boy could sleep on. The girl could hear the woman, her mother, replying to the man in the bed. *No, not again*, the mother's voice could seem to say, *not with the children here*—a thudding sound could occur, which the girl would hear not with her ears but in her hand and wrist and directly, thuddingly, in the center of her chest. The woman could choke off a sob. The couple could slip out of the room onto the balcony, while the muffled sobs of the woman swept back to the girl like a lullaby, the soft carving of her mother's fingernails into her wrist. The girl could begin to silently come apart upon the floor, drifting limb by limb through the roof of the hotel room. The boy could sleep on, not knowing he would be wakened by a kick that would send him weeping to the corner of the room, clutching the sheet to his head. He could sleep on at the foot of the bed, and the girl could lie awake feeling the soft carving of her mother's nails in her wrist, lulled by the croon of the woman's strangled sobbing not into sleep but into a wakefulness more deep and absent than slumber. The man could continue to grunt, the woman to sob, the boy to sleep within the circumference of only a creosote bush. A creosote bush is large enough for these things, even if they should continue for years.

It is unusual to find a creosote bush growing in solitude. In most areas, they cluster over the acres like family. But whether a creosote lives alone or in the company of its kin, it is not impossible for a single specimen to contain a small throng of women, forming unannounced before daybreak. Many weeping women could begin to circle, around and around without pausing, careless of the absence of landmarks by which to count their passage. Their headscarves could slowly drench with perspiration, and their eyes could begin to glaze with thirst. Thirst for their sons. Somewhere nearby, their sons could be slit from nipple to nipple not once but many times and soaked with alcohol. Each nipple could be gouged away, could be doused again with alcohol not once but many times. Filaments fine as thread and carrying volts of pain undreamed could be placed at their scrotums, at the delicate spider-egg sacs webbed with blue that the women sponged each day for years, dreaming of smooth-faced young brides and the soft cries of grandchildren.

The women could stumble shoulder to shoulder, describing arc after arc, weeping or stone-eyed at the mindsight of the guards smoking in the corridor, each waiting his turn at the girls inside, at the daughters of the women. Thirteen, seventeen years old. Girls. Finished, the guards could slide their muzzles there, could unload six quick rounds into the furrow, stopping afterward in the yard to rinse the blood and sperm. First a girl, her younger sister watching, and then the younger sister. The mothers circle and circle. They cannot contain this. For each it happens at a different time: each body breaks open, each soul slides silky wet up the white Sonora sky. One by one they shatter, *Give me madness, Jesus, show me your sweet face*, gliding up invincible now while below their frames still stagger circling like broken birds. All this could, theoretically, occur within a space no larger than a single creosote bush, the roots of which would not shrink from the soil.

These things are true: the grace of the willow on the streambank.

The blue spruce splendoring behind the cabin.

Mountainfuls of maple forest after frost.

Neither you nor I would be the one to deny these things.

Yet observe for a moment the grace of the creosote bush, hollowing as it grows, stretching and bending under an empty sky. Wind, scorch, thirst—years of these things. Centuries. How it endures. And then—a swelling secretly open, a burgeoning lack, a pregnancy of sorrow, until at long last you fall to your knees before the weeping child . . . the spread trembling fingers of the derelict . . . the deathbed shudder of the beloved stranger . . . and you cry *Here it is!*, speaking of your self as of a jar or a bowl, offering and offering your last fiber, your last salt breath, each terrified pulse of you as a sacrament to you know not what.

Farm Use

After the divorce, my mother's first entrepreneurial effort fails. She opens a resale clothing shop and gives it a clever name: Encore. But in small-town West Virginia, people's used finery is a shabby thing. Her clientele has none of the chic-girl-down-on-her-luck wit the name deserves; instead of Jean Rhys heroines, she attracts fat, bad-smelling women who slap their kids. There is nothing vintage to find. Her racks hold only the same clothes that once hung at Hill's and Heck's, the budget department stores. But dingier, with the smell of stale closets. At the counter, irritated women claim their things are worth more than my mother thinks.

Even in the black-and-white wedding photos, my mother's eyes have a touch of come-hither glint. My father's face is young, eager, shining. He looks toward her, but she looks only at the camera, chin lowered, one white satin toe pointed forward, eyes leveling their invitation.

Once she and some other stewardesses partied on a yacht with

O. J. Simpson, she tells me when I'm nine. I think how much fun it would be: throwing footballs on the deck, eating cake all day.

His hands are furred black, his head bald and shiny, his gut a fat ball under graying t-shirts. He buys my brother Tonka trucks, buys me the radio I crave, buys my mother clothes and me a plum velvet blazer, very grown-up, for wearing to the Kingdom Hall. "Won't it be nice," my mother purrs, "to use the child support your father sends just on school clothes and nice things, instead of bills?"

She's got us there. I'm sick of food stamps and government cheese and clothes discarded by strangers. Middle school is a bad time to be poor. And I'm tall for my age and pretty. At assemblies, eighteen-year-old brothers from other congregations flirt with me between sessions, ask my mother if they can take me out. They back away, apologizing, when they learn I'm twelve. I want a black leather clutch purse and combs for my hair.

But not this way. I argue with her, but things move quickly. He makes fourteen dollars an hour working construction. He's a respected brother; he's served at Bethel. A date is set. I'm to wear my plum velvet blazer. My brother, seven, is to give her away in the ceremony at our Kingdom Hall.

"Won't that be cute?" she says.

"No, not really," I say.

I cry in her room as she dresses, begging her not to do it, but I have no evidence aside from the weird way he looks at us. She's patient for a while, going over the money he makes, the good reputation he has in his congregation—but finally she turns on me.

"I am just about fed up, you hear? Do you understand me? I've just about had it with your bellyaching." She swings the hairbrush in my face. "Why do you always want to ruin everything? Why? One good thing comes along, something that will actually make me happy for once, and you have to start your whining. As usual."

"He's not a good man." I'm still crying. She laughs angrily, throws the brush down on the bureau.

"What do you know about good men? You're twelve years old." Her voice is rich with disgust. "Do you think you know what a good man is? Do you?" She shakes me. "Well?" I just cry. "Do you think your *father's* a good man?"

I look at the brown and green carpet. "Yes."

She stares at me, then lets me loose with a final shake and turns her back. She steps into the silky fawn dress.

"Well, that just shows what you know." It's early in the day, but the wide straps of her bra are already gouging into her shoulders, scoring the red welts we see when she changes into her nightgown at night. She tosses her head, talks to the mirror. "You listen here. I'm getting married today, and there's nothing, absolutely nothing, that you can do about it. Do you hear me?"

"Yes."

"For your information, young lady, I am happy. You can be happy, too, or you can sit in the corner and snivel. Is that clear?"

"Yes."

When the elder asks, "Who gives this woman in marriage?" my brother, confused, must be prodded to speak. "I do," he says, worried, his eyes casting about to see if he's done the right thing.

The promised wealth does not materialize. Our stepfather visits numerous doctors until one agrees to sign the papers that say he has black lung. He has bullied our mother into selling her share of the store, into selling our house, into buying a trailer and moving hours away to a trailer park in a small town where we know no one.

The first disability check arrives. He stops working, stays home. He's constantly there, watching.

The money problems worsen. Our clothes are not replaced. We start the new school shabby, in castoffs. If we want clothes for school, he tells us, we can have a yard sale, sell our toys. Our mother urges us to comply; we'll feel so much better if we have some nice things.

All Saturday we sit in the yard. Strange kids pick up my horse models, my brother's Matchbox cars and Tonka trucks. One by one the items go, my plastic family of smoke-gray Arabians scattered.

We make almost a hundred dollars. It can buy new shoes for both of us, new pants for my brother, maybe a sweater for me.

Our stepfather takes the stack of ones. There will be no clothes. Everything that's ours, he says, is his. Get used to it.

We go to school ragged, mismatched, hopeless.

In rural areas, the occasional truck has *Farm Use* painted on its sides, a special dispensation to relieve the family farm of the expenses of a license, insurance.

In the back, sometimes, gaunt children ride, their arms wrapped tiredly around their knees, hunched amid hay bales or firewood or piles of scrap. They stare dead-eyed into the car behind.

My brother and I are those children, our arms wrapped around our bent legs. We've moved out to unimproved acreage, and our step-father drives our Farm Use truck all over town: to the post office, the grocery. We sit in the back, staring at children belted safely into seats beside their parents. Sometimes, they're children from school, children we know. They point, talk to their parents excitedly, stare at us in fascination and disgust.

My ass is a moving target. That's what he calls it, *ass*, a word we're not allowed to say. I cannot pass the couch without a slap, a pinch, a long stroke that ends in squeezing. I walk as quickly, straightly, as invisibly as I can.

"This girl of yours sure does love to wiggle, don't she, Mother?" he calls to the kitchen.

"Yes, she does," comes a deadened voice.

As time passes, the rules intensify. Work is a punishment; after school, we clear brush until we cannot see to sickle. We carry wood, dig ditches for the gas lines. Food becomes a measured thing. Each mealtime, my stepfather dishes himself up from the pots. Then my mother may help herself to half of what he has taken. Then, while he watches, she can spoon half of what she's taken onto my plate. A portion half the size of mine goes to my brother. If my stepfather wants one peanut butter and jelly sandwich, my brother gets one-eighth. If she gives us more than our stepfather calculates is correct, he beats my brother with his belt.

We sit at dinner, our eyes on our plates. If we look our stepfather in the eye, ever, without being told to, we're beaten.

"How those little titties of yours doing?" he says to me. "They must be sprouting pretty good right about now."

If I do not keep eating, I'll have stomach pains later, or I'll have to eat dry the packets of Carnation Instant Breakfast we all get free in gym and that the other girls leave lying in their lockers. After class, I try to make my voice casual. "Are you going to eat that?" I say, pointing.

They look at each other, grinning. Then back at me, their eyes cool and repelled. "No. My god. Take it if you want it."

You're supposed to pour it in milk, but I have no milk. On the school bus, I sink down so no one can see me as I rip the top back, pour the dry grains in my mouth, chew the moistening wads of sweet powder. I learn to like it.

"Must be like two puppies. Isn't that right, Mother?"

"Yes."

"Two puppies with brown noses."

Something in my throat is clogging, but I chew, eyes down, head down. My brother keeps eating. I feel my mother's gaze like a beam of heat in my hair.

Doing dishes, I palm a steak knife from the kitchen, easing the drawer silently open, sliding it into my pocket. In bed, I slide it under the side pillow, practice grabbing it in the dark, my hand darting to catch its handle.

He finds it, lying beside me in the darkness as he has begun to do, breathing, his whole body still and heavy in the bed next to me. First, on top of the bedspread. Now under the sheets.

I think of nothing. I do not pray. I lie there in a stillness so extreme I might be dead, each nerve a wire humming with still terror.

"What's this?" he says. He sits up. "Turn that light on." I do. The room jumps to brightness, and I pull my arm back to my side. Only my eyes swerve to see the knife gripped in his hand.

"What you got this for, girly?"

I look at the window, the door, long for my mother to appear. "It's so isolated here. I get afraid. Of robbers, I mean." My voice is strangled, unbelievable.

"Is that so?" His grin leaks slowly across his mouth. It's a good game, cat and mouse. "Robbers."

"Yes. It's isolated here," I say.

"Well, no robbers are gonna get you. I'm here. I'm here to protect my little girl. You don't need this." He rises and moves around the bed to stand above me. "We don't want you cutting yourself by accident, do we? A sharp knife like this?" He holds the blade in my face. I push my head back into the pillow.

"No, sir," I whisper.

"Then I'll just take this back to the kitchen." Quick as a fox, his free hand reaches out and flips back the blankets, unzips my quilted pink nightgown, sternum to crotch, flips the fabric open. He stares down at me, my breasts, my hipbones, my white underwear. His eyes glitter. He grins down for a minute.

"So cover yourself up," he says. My hands fly to my waist, but the zipper snags, sticks, jerks upward. "Don't be so modest," he laughs.

"Fathers have the right to see their daughters. It's natural." The corners of the room are thick with shadow. "And what am I?"

"My spiritual father," I whisper. I am a wax doll, empty, pliant, a cunning image of the girl who used to live here.

"That's right." The lamp clicks. The darkness becomes deeper darkness. "No more knives. You hear?"

"Yes, sir."

His steps shake the trailer as he moves down the hall.

The way to make my stepfather a pie is this. First, you make the crust, the light, flaking, curling crust he requires every day. My mother does this with her family recipe and sets it aside. I meet her at the table in the yard, each of us holding a small knife.

Then you peel the apples—the small, sweet ones, the kind he likes; I don't know what they're called: I'm not allowed in the grocery store—and then you cut them in half, top to bottom, straight through the center. Then you cut the halves in half. Then you scoop the core out with the knife, following the lines in the apple's pale meat. Then you slice the cored quarters.

The slices will go into the crust, and the dish will go into the oven. Two pieces, hot, will go into their bowls, and his will get a scoop of Breyer's vanilla ice cream, which he tells us many times is the best ice cream, as BMW is the best motorbike and Nikon is the best camera. Both of which he has. "Bavarian Motor Works," he likes to bellow, apropos of nothing.

My brother and I do not eat pie. It is a punishment. "Five desserts!" our stepfather yells when we err, leaping triumphantly to his feet to make the little marks, ┼┼┼, on the sheet pinned to the wall for that purpose. When I run away, I am up to minus seventy-six desserts. We never get to zero. When we get close, he's more watchful. He loves to let us get down to two or three.

It's fall. He's inside watching television. My mother and I sit in the yard, peeling, coring, slicing. The glossy apples disappear under our knives, emerge as neat pale slivers lying flat in the dish. I feel the slight resistance of the flesh, then the final quick *thunk* as the blade hits board.

"I don't know what I'm going to do," she says in a low smothered voice.

I carve a red curling spiral away from the flesh.

She glances at me, sighs noisily. "I just don't know what I'm going to do."

"What about?"

"About him."

I think she's going to talk about running again. I'm sick of running, sick of waking up in the motel bed to hear her whispering into the phone, promising, apologizing, giving him directions. I'm sick of the pains in my stomach when we head back east again. Maybe she's starting to plan, I think. But we have no second car to run in now. He sold it after the last time. There's no money for Greyhound tickets. We're twelve miles outside a little town in rural West Virginia. We know no one but Witnesses.

And we've been through that, spent nights at elders' houses, her face bearing the marks of beatings, my brother bruised and shaking, the two of us huddled silent on a strange couch. They send us home. It's a family situation, a private matter. They acknowledge the rule my stepfather holds over her like a swinging blade: Except in cases of adultery, a wife cannot divorce her husband. It's a sin. We go back.

But leaving isn't on her mind.

"I don't know what it's going to take." My quarters fall into clean fans of slices, which I gather and drop in the dish.

"What what's going to take?"

"What it's going to take to satisfy him."

My knife steadies itself against the board. "Meaning what?"

"He's never satisfied." Her voice drops to a whisper. "Nothing I do." She pushes a long lock of gray back from her face. All the curl's fallen out of it since he made her grow it out. "Three, four times a day he wants it."

I cut my last apple through its center.

"You're a big girl. You know what I mean."

The halves into halves. The half-moons of the cores, the pith and seeds into the pot of waste.

"I could lose my mind," she says, her voice breaking. I stop cutting and look up. She's crying, but her hands don't stop moving. I can hear the creek. My brother is scything weeds in the distance. "I think it might kill me or something." She keeps her eyes on her apple, her knife. The trees rise dark up the mountain behind her. "He needs some other kind of—some kind of outlet." The only sound is her knife hitting the board as the slices separate.

I stare at her, at the wide dark bowl of the valley we live in. She glances up at me, then at the dish of apples.

"Here, have one," she says, fishing out a slice. Even though apples have been forbidden to my brother and me for months, I can re-member their taste, their sour springing juice. She shakes it at me anxiously, glances at the trailer windows. For him to see this would mean a beating—for me, at least, if not for her.

"I think I'm done," I say, and stand up.

Hip Joints

In the late afternoon of the twentieth century, after Vietnam and before Anita Hill, in the Appalachian highlands of rural West Virginia, it was senior year, and Madonna and the Police filled the airwaves: "Like a Virgin," "King of Pain."

Every noon, I drove the six miles from East Fairmont High School to the little machine shop tucked on a winding back road. I'd park in the gravel lot and let the car battery run the radio while I ate my brown-bagged tuna sandwich and stared out the windshield. My classmates at East Fairmont were dissecting little dead animals and solving for y.

I was done with all that; I was impatient; I had all the credits I needed to graduate. I took morning classes so the state wouldn't charge me with truancy, and then I left for work.

"I machine artificial hip joints for 3M," I would say when people asked.

It was tedious, it was eight hours every weekday, it was just the whir of machines for company, the other workers attending silently to their own stations. But at least it wasn't McDonald's or Dairy Queen; I didn't have to wait on people from high school. And it beat minimum wage by a couple of dollars an hour. Sixteen years old, forty hours a week: I felt lucky.

The titanium hip joints were pocked with small regular holes; they looked like halves of silver Wiffle balls. Titanium: strong and light, sleek and durable, a perfect metal for aerospace engineering or replacing the worn interiors of human bodies. I'd imagine the gloved hands of surgeons inserting the shining silver balls into the dark slick privacies of the pelvis.

In the shop, the machines were huge teal cubes, large and clean, twice as tall as I was, with hot moving steel parts at their hearts where I put my hands to lock down and then remove the half-balls. The machines all had red warning labels that showed how you could die or lose a limb.

While one piece was whirring, I squirted coolant on it, or I scraped the little razor-sharp curls, which we called burrs, off the edges of the previously finished piece. Then I lined it up in its row on the tray of the rolling metal table. When the tray was full, I rolled it over to the next station, where a man or woman stood, heavy and silent, staring into another machine.

On my breaks, I sat cross-legged on the hood of my dad's old red Chevy and watched the sky darken. I drank my cold bottle of Tab and pondered the future. I was earning money, I was going to be the first in my family to go to college, and it was getting well on into spring. One month to graduation, then three more months' earnings in the summer. As soon as I graduated, I could pull overtime; the boss liked me. He always smiled and said, "Everything ducky?" when he walked by my station, and I always said yes. I'd been raised not to complain, not to ask questions, to be obedient to authority and grateful for the opportunity to work.

And it was a good job. Steady. Though the building was windowless and the tasks were dull, on warm days the boss would open the big garage doors that faced onto the truck docks, and we could see the trees and sky and the little houses farther on down the valley.

The boss, who owned everything, spent most of his time in the carpeted office with the Xerox machine and the phone and the receptionist who passed out the checks every two weeks. He kept his hands clean.

More than twenty years later, I cannot remember the receptionist's face, only her graying brown sausage curls, the striped t-shirts she wore that clung tight to her middle. And I can't remember the faces of the other workers, either, although they were there, scraping off their own burrs with tiny flathead screwdrivers and wheeling their own metal carts to and fro, smoking their cigarettes during breaks out on the cement slab. I can recall the boss, with his squashed nose and gray hair, who was kind and seemed amused that a high-school girl heading for college wanted to work in his small factory with adults who worked there full-time, supporting families.

"National Merit," he'd said, pushing his glasses up with a squat finger, reading through my application. "Sounds like something special." Sometimes he'd ask me what the book stuffed in my back pocket was, and I'd pull it out and hand it to him. He'd tap the cover. "Oh, yeah," he'd say. "I heard of this guy." He'd hand it back. "Only on breaks, hear?" he'd say.

"Only on breaks," I'd agree. I remember him well.

But clearest of all, more than twenty years later, is the floor manager, a tall guy—I'll call him Gary—with his sagging football-star body and bowl-cut brown hair. He was always riding me, checking my pieces, timing my output. His eyes were brown and sad, and I'd thought at first I could like him. Sometimes he'd joke around, and I'd want to laugh, but the jokes weren't funny. They were always racist or at someone's expense, and his laugh sounded wrong, harsh, urgent in its need for agreement, like the laughter of the jocks at school who taunted special-ed kids in the parking lot. If you didn't laugh along, they'd turn on you. It was best to walk away. Teachers never intervened, never protected the fat girl they called "Hair-Bear" or the lopsided boy who always got tripped.

At the factory, the regulars would knock off every night at six, and the receptionist and the boss would close up the office. They'd all go home to their families and dinners. I stayed late to get the hours, and Gary the floor manager did, too.

The big cement room would shine weirdly in the fluorescent buzz, the machines' intricate stainless-steel centers glistening with lube, the mopped floor quickly drying. The boss let me work until eight-thirty, which gave me a full shift, and Gary, angling for a raise—whose "whole damn *life* is this shop, man," as he'd declare, passionately, whenever the boss was around—stayed to close it down. He'd work on another machine or sit at a table in the corner, doing paperwork.

At eight-thirty, I would drive home tired in the red Chevy and hug my dad and stepmom and little brother. I'd heat up a plate of whatever had been dinner and sit at the kitchen counter, doing my homework, and say good night when they headed for bed.

When I finished, I'd call Mike or my friend Michelle and talk for a while, lying on the kitchen floor with my feet up the wall and winding the long curly phone cord around my wrist. On weekends, we'd double-date at the movies or the pizza place at the mall with Michelle's current boyfriend. Afterward, Mike and I would drive alone in his parents' blue Jeep Wagoneer to the strip mine. We'd park and talk about how we'd definitely stay together after I left for college: how we'd write a lot and talk on the phone and eventually maybe he could move to Texas and we could get an apartment. I'd lie warm in his letter jacket and listen while the white stars shifted a little. We'd fold the rubbers into McDonald's wrappers.

After twenty years, the memory of Mike is still clear: his kind, believing eyes, his steady muscles. He married a local girl and started a gym. On rare visits home to my folks, I would hear fragments of news about him.

At the corner of the hip joint factory, there was a little room that I'd never been inside, but one night Gary came up and stood behind me.

I was leaning halfway into the big teal machine, squirting coolant to keep the sparks down. At first, I didn't even hear him.

"Hey, I've got something new for you," he said loudly, and I startled upward, banging my head. Wincing, I pulled out from the hulking metal.

I rubbed my skull. "What?"

"I got some fine machining that needs done, and I think maybe you got the experience now to handle it."

"Okay," I said, following him, wiping my hands on the pink shop-rag. He went into the little room and flipped on the overhead light.

On top of wide tables, small machines squatted, their metal skins painted a glossy beige. They had silver parts at their centers like the big machines did, but they looked simpler, like a less evolved species. Their pale cords snaked limply to the wall.

He picked up a hip joint and stabbed his finger at the slight bump that protruded at the crest of its roundedness, a tiny mound you could feel.

"You see that thing?"

"Yeah."

"You know what that is?"

I hesitated. "A bump?"

He roared with disgust and laughter. "No, College. That ain't no bump." He poked at it. "That there's a *nipple*. A nipple. You got that?"

"Yeah. Okay."

"So what is it?"

I swallowed. "A nipple."

"Right. And this here"—he flipped the switch of a machine, and a large, vertical stone wheel started to spin—"is a nipple-grinder." His grip on the thin edges of the half-ball was surprisingly delicate. He pressed the metal hard against the rough stone edge. "You got to hold it steady," he said, frowning, "so it rubs the nipple good." He checked it, pressed it back against the grindstone, checked it again.

The titanium was perfectly smooth. He shoved it triumphantly toward my face. "See that?" he said. "Presto. No more nipple."

I nodded.

"Now you do it." He handed me one from a tray. "Go on."

He stood behind me as I worked, and I began to feel the soft heat of his paunch radiating against my back. I frowned intently, as he had, and shifted as though to get a better angle, and his body did not follow mine. I kept my piece pressed to the grindstone, my wrists vibrating, and then held up the piece for his gaze.

"Huh," he said. His brown eyes were sullen. "That's pretty good. That'll do." He waved at the full tray. "You do these, you can go home."

"I go home at eight-thirty," I said.

"You go home when you finish." He walked out of the room.

I sighed, the tension rippling out of me, and picked up the next one. I felt shy for the shining little mounds, and afraid. I wanted to cover them all with a soft pink shop-rag and let them sleep. Instead I stood before the wheel, scraping off the little bumps, wondering why they had to be called nipples, wondering why men were so gross—why, when you were helping your father put the stereo together, things that got shoved into other things were called male, and the parts that waited with open holes were called female, and he said it so simply, so benignly, and he was my father who loved me and would never dream of hurting me, not the stepfather who'd beaten me and touched me and from whose trailer I'd run away. So who had made that up, that female-hole thing? And why did I seem to be the only person disturbed and embarrassed by it? It hurt my stomach, it felt like a slap or a blow, but no one else seemed even to notice, or if they did, like the boys in shop class, they thought it was funny and titterworthy, like a dirty joke.

It was not that I was a prude. In the blue Wagoneer's backseat, I got on top, I sucked Mike off with the tricks I read about in my stepmother's *Cosmopolitan*, I hooked my heel on the front-seat headrest and spanned out my flexible legs so he could see and touch and lick me. I wasn't ashamed, and I wasn't timid. I refused to let myself stay stunned and fazed by what my stepfather had done. Sex wouldn't master me; I would master it.

But I wasn't a piece or a hole, either. I wasn't a machine that just anyone could switch on, or a part they could handle and scrape.

I lined the hip joints neatly in their rows: they were little silver half-Wiffle balls. Anyone could see that. Not breasts. They went into the hips of hurt people and helped them walk again. Why did everything have to be a tit or a dick or a hole?

I finished the tray by eight-thirty, slipped out without speaking, and drove home fast on the dark curves.

So it went on like that. The other factory workers would leave at six, flipping their hands in brusque goodbyes from the open garage doors as the spring wore on. They'd bend and let gravity suck them down off the cement docks to the gravel, and their truck engines would gun and they'd drive away. Then the shop would echo with the hum of just two machines, Gary's and mine, and the buzz of the fluorescent tubes overhead, and the slap of his footfalls on the cement when he went to check on something. And night after night, when the trees turned black against the rose-colored sky and the wind blew in full of spring smells, his large hand would fall on my shoulder or the small of my back.

"Got some work for you," he'd say, and he'd walk behind me to the little room. "What are we gonna do tonight?"

"Grind nipples." I'd just say it. Arguing was boring, pointless.

"That's right. We're gonna grind us some nipples." He'd pick up the first one and put it in my hand, flip on the machine, and steer me in front of it. "You ready to grind?"

"Yes."

"Yes, what?"

I knew the phrase he wanted. "Yes, I'm ready to grind nipples."

"Then grind, College. Grind till those nipples are history." And he'd watch for a while as I held my wrists steady, and then he'd leave, and I'd hate him until eight-thirty, working fast, thinking *Five-fifty an hour, five-fifty an hour.*

I had almost enough saved up in my account to pay for room and board, which the scholarship in Texas wouldn't cover. "We're proud of you, honey," my dad had said. "But college is for rich people's kids. If you want it, you're going to have to find a way to pay for it, okay?"

It was no big deal. After living with my mother and stepfather in the trailer, where we ate dry pancakes for dinner and wore strangers' clothes dug out of trash bags, it had always been easy to do without things other kids expected: a class ring, fancy clothes. My father's house was peaceful, and he loved me, and that was enough. Everything went into the savings account.

One warm summer night after graduation, working in the little room, smoothing off the small bumps, I didn't hear Gary come back in. His voice was sudden and rough at the back of my neck. "How long you gonna make me wait?"

My hands jerked in surprise, and the wheel skinned the flesh off my left knuckles. A thin red thread whipped around on the grinding edge.

I turned slowly to face him, my back to the wheel, my hands holding the hip joint out in front of me like a tiny shield.

"How long?" he said.

I could feel the wheel's air moving at my spine, a breeze through my t-shirt.

I didn't look in his eyes. My stepfather had taught me that much. "I don't know what you're talking about."

He smiled and spread his hands in the air between us. "What are you looking so scared for?"

"I'm not scared."

"Well, maybe you ought to be," he said, and his smile disappeared to wherever it had come from. "Nobody here but us. Doors are all

Hip Joints   43

shut." His brown eyes looked sly, and I curled and uncurled my toes inside my shoes to inch backward, but then I could feel the cotton of my shirt blown soft against my spine all along the length of the spinning vertical wheel.

"I know you go with them high school boys," he said, leaning closer, and I said nothing. I arched backward so I wouldn't hit the spinning stone. His hand reached for my ribs.

"It's eight-thirty," I said, staring up at the seam where the ceiling joined the wall. "I need to go home." Flexing backward, my hips started to quiver with the strain. The grindstone spun.

"Even if you scream, no one can hear you," he said, and I could smell the orange Fanta on his breath. One part of my brain wanted to laugh, wanted to ask him if he'd gotten his lines from a bad TV movie, but I couldn't. I couldn't breathe, and the whole room was swimming and going dark around the edges.

"My dad's expecting me," I said. "If I'm not home on time, he'll come looking." It wasn't true—I could stay out as late as I wanted—and I was no good at lying.

But Gary's hand stilled, and then he slowly backed away. I straightened up, my eyes skimming past him.

"I never did anything," he said.

I edged around him, not breathing, and moved toward the door. Slipping into the larger room, I began to run, and I tore through the door and onto the dock, leaping down onto the gravel in one stride with my car keys already in my hand.

I took the long way home up the interstate until my hands stopped shaking on the wheel. Billy Idol wailed about white weddings against the warm, dark wind.

At home, I unlocked the front door with my key. My parents and brother were out somewhere. I lifted the lid of the pot on the stove. I ate what was left and did my homework and went to bed without calling anyone, but the next day from the phone in the kitchen, I called the receptionist to say I quit.

"Huh," she said. "Well, honey, you quit without giving notice like that, the boss keeps your last check."

"I know," I said. "Keep it."

For a while I told my family I just needed some extra time after graduation to get things tied up, college forms and such, and they nodded, not knowing what college involved. Then I told everyone I would definitely be getting another job soon. But I didn't. I didn't even look for one, and I told no one about what had happened in the machine shop. *Sexual harassment* was not a phrase I knew. Maybe all men were like that, or maybe there was something about me that magnetized the crazy ones.

Back when I lived in the trailer, I had gone to my mother and told her about what my stepfather had done, the weird touching in my bed at night, and she had called me a liar. Said I was imagining things, too sensitive. I ran away, and I didn't try telling anyone about the touching again. When I testified, I stuck to the beatings and the starving, and the police and the courts got my little brother out.

Now we lived with my dad, and he loved us but didn't like to hear about any of it. It made him too sad.

So I told no one about the floor manager's threats. I spent most of that summer just hanging out, mostly at home, watching movies on the new VCR or sitting under the backyard trees. Sometimes I read books, and sometimes I just stared at the green leaves shifting.

"You can't just sit around like this, Joy," my dad would say, reminding me of the money I still needed to earn, and I'd agree and apologize and drift off to my room.

"Well, don't ask me," I could hear him saying to my stepmother down the hall. "She's not a lazy girl." Like most Latinos in places as white as West Virginia, my father always carried, I think, a mild anxiety about proving ourselves, about not seeming lazy to the good, hardworking citizens who surrounded us. "I don't know what's the matter with her."

No one did. I didn't go to the mall with Michelle anymore, and I didn't feel like driving at night with Mike up to the strip mine.

Sometimes, though, I would walk there alone during the day, picking my way along the bumpy brown clods of earth, the crickets' hot drone falling and lifting in waves. I would stare at the bared bands of the earth's interior, its uncovered layers of dark and light, the thin veins of black shine the miners dug for and the worthless brown dirt they pushed aside.

Whole tops of mountains had been scraped away. On the stripped plateaus, I'd squat and finger the flat bland grass that grew back smooth and green and thin.

I would walk and stare and sweat until a hot numbing daze fell over me and all I could feel was thirst, and the crickets' drone made me peaceful and sleepy and I could turn at last and head for home.

But I only liked to go on the weekends, when all the men were gone and the big machines sat idle, waiting.

No *Más* Monkey

And some of our soldiers even asked whether the things
that we saw were not a dream?

—Bernal Díaz del Castillo, *The Conquest of New Spain*

I thanked you but didn't really like the earrings you'd made. Their
dangling glass seed beads of white and turquoise looked cheap, their
strange geometry ugly to me.

Drunk, I didn't know how to feel your soft mouth on me, softer
than a man's. In on your scheme, our boyfriends stayed away, buying
beer forever, while you tried a thing you'd only seen in Jack's magazines. I moved in your musk like a clockwork toy—to be polite, to
prove I could.

"I *like* my makeup," you said, when people suggested that you tone
it down: your glossy maroon lips, your kohl-rimmed eyes, your brown
cheerleader's body cased in leopard spandex, the fake lacquered over
the real.

In the Thunderbird Apartments, we lived together: you, me, your boyfriend, mine, all feral, all under twenty. You read *Pet Sematary* and believed in demons, crows as omens, *curanderas* and the Catholic Church. I went to college and believed in nothing. We folded our laundry together, the comfort of cloth, soft and warm, clean, the lemon-pink scent of mimosa trees blowing in sweet. San Antonio, spring.

But you were hard, a runaway like me. When we watched *The Fly* on cable TV, and the telepod failed, twisting the baboon's insides out to its skin, you said flatly, "No *más* monkey." Hysterical, stoned, we couldn't stop saying it.

Later you had a daughter and got fat. Jack sold cocaine, then left. When I visited, you had a new guy, nice, who didn't smack you. Our kids played while you talked about how much your furniture cost, how you found dressers dumped on the curb, cleaned them, painted over their pasts. You said we'd always be friends; I only smiled. I was in grad school then.

In Mexico City with other professors, I stopped, shocked, at the glass case in the Museo Nacional de Antropología that held earrings just like the ones you'd made me, but ancient Aztec, dug up at the seat of your empire, Cindy, an empire you never saw. Same shape, same size, same design. I pressed my fingertips to the glass, breathing hard as if I'd been running or hurt. I wanted to show you the scale model of Tenochtitlán: the blue water, the bridges, the islands, the aqueducts, the intricately engineered causeways where ten horses could trot side by side, the thousands of canoes, the glory Europeans couldn't fathom, the lake they drained, the temples they buried.

But you were dead, smashed by four teenagers taking a red light at eighty in an SUV: Houston, 2000, RIP.

Only the world tree links us now, its roots with you, its trunk with me, its branches in the heavens where gods require blood sacrifice and prayer and speak a language we can't understand.

Chac-Mool, here's my heart.

It's pouring out.

I didn't know how to see what you gave me, Cindy, how to wear what you wanted to adorn me with. They've lain in a drawer these many years, quiet in the dark. When I open it, they flash like water.

Edging

When the baby was born, Jeff and I were living in a barrio in San Antonio. I was two years from graduating, and he worked nights as a security guard at a power plant making $650 a month. Two hundred dollars rented a makeshift apartment in an old two-story house, with a chin-high General Motors refrigerator that needed weekly defrosting and an oven you could light only with a rolled-up newspaper. It was 1988, and we were dirt poor.

The most pervasive memory I have of that time is the sense of insecurity—the screaming and slamming in the apartment below: Adam and Diana, nineteen and eighteen, with a two-year-old daughter and a newborn son, all wedged into a kitchen, bath, and bedroom with no air-conditioning, one rattling fan. Or the night Jeff ran into the street with his gun tucked into his jeans while I stood on the terrace dialing 911 and hushing Grey on my hip: a woman screaming rape down the block. (Shrieking at the cops, "Don't leave me here! Don't *leave* me!" after they had taken her report, the car pulling slowly from the curb, the officer's profile flashing red and blue as he shook his thick face at her.) Not being able to play in the yard with Grey: scraps of metal embedded in the dirt, hidden beneath grass; beer can shims silvering the driveway, broken glass lacing the sidewalk cracks, old rubbers shimmering under the stairs. The tense conversations every two weeks when we decided which bills to pay and which to put off with a token five dollars. Or in line at the checkout counter, waiting until the last possible moment to pull out the food stamps, not looking in anyone's face. The pathetic guilt when we borrowed coins from the baby's piggy bank to do laundry.

How the glossy parenting magazine came to be in the apartment I don't remember. Magazines were a luxury we didn't buy. I flipped eagerly to an article on how young mothers could find more time for themselves, but its recommendations bore no resemblance to my life. When it cheerfully informed me I didn't need to iron my family's t-shirts, I sat down laughing. As if I ironed t-shirts. As if we owned an iron.

Where was the article telling me I didn't need to lug the baby and his diaper bag downtown on the bus to the free clinic and spend hours waiting for immunizations? Or didn't need to ride across town to sit for hours with other mothers and their children in a room, waiting to be lectured by the social worker so I could get the WIC cards that gave us orange juice and milk? But I did.

The dean of students—herself middle aged, single, and childless—had permitted me a maternity leave of only two weeks: delivery, recovery, bonding, adjustment, back to class. We couldn't afford daycare, didn't have relatives close by to help. Jeff slept during the days, worked nights. We handed off the baby like a baton, spoke little. I typed papers while I nursed.

At Christmas we visited friends just for the evening, and when we returned our pipes had frozen and broken. Icy slush across the torn linoleum. (Two old gas heaters, neither with a grate: we had to turn them off when we left for fear of fire. Eleven houses burned down in the two years we lived in that neighborhood—arson, vagrants, badly equipped buildings like ours.) We stayed for three nights in one of the guest rooms of a student friend—a whole house to himself in Alamo Heights while he finished college, a sixth-year junior, living off family money. Looking not quite at me, at a spot above the wide-screen TV: "I mean, it's nothing about *you* guys, it's just the *baby*, you know. He just gets on my—well, he's just so *active*, you know. I mean, I guess one more night would be okay, but after that, well, I mean I'm sure y'all have lots of other friends that wouldn't mind—" and us with sixty-four cents between us. He left to buy a quarter bag and rent a couple of movies, and the two of us sat numbly on the sofa, saying nothing, until Grey toddled over and we felt guilty at the worry in his little face.

Insecurity, yes, and bitterness too. And fear like an old coin in the side of your mouth—so familiar you forget, and then a wash of metal floods your tongue.

Two blocks away was the Stop-n-Go where we'd sometimes buy milk, and every payday two cold lemonades, sitting on the curb with all the *vatos* and their beer, laughing at the funny things Grey did. Next door was the big air-conditioned laundromat where we did wash on Sundays.

It happened on a miserably hot, bright, humid day, around 108 degrees. We had lingered over the folding for the coolness, taking turns pushing the baby around in the wheeled baskets between the rows of washers, the faded plastic plants. It had been quiet when we left.

We saw it on the news that night and in the newspaper the next day. A little boy and his father were standing together on the sidewalk in front of the store with their paper cups of Coke, talking. A woman pulled in to get iced tea. Did her foot slip from the brake to the accelerator? Did a sudden spasm in her leg make her slam it down? She couldn't say. She couldn't speak to the microphone waving in her face. She couldn't speak: her car jumped the curb and severed the child in half against the lower shelf edge of a phone booth. His father wasn't two feet away.

After graduation, we moved to east Texas and rented a small wooden house in the country near the town where the grad school was. Horses sauntered up to the fence and lipped sliced apples from our hands. The days and nights were quiet. But I could not stop imagining that father's helplessness, the emptiness of the arms that weren't fast enough. The punishment that was not going to end: the edges would rub and rub and one day be soft, but soft like the shape of a mouth that opens to moan, and smeared the way edges of objects blur just before tears. A grief like the fish in the bottom of the boat that won't stop gasping long enough to die, and you hate it for not dying, for making you watch it helplessly flopping. And then when it dies you double up on the floor of the boat and wail.

This morning in the pre-dawn hours after putting my bandaged son to bed, I stand alone in the dark living room, staring into the greater darkness outside. Before bedtime, I'd been brushing my teeth when he'd rushed in to show me a drawing, and I turned to look—and instead, as if in terrible slow motion, saw him spin and fall, smashing his face on the rim of the porcelain tub. Saw the chin, the neck, the chest drenched in blood, the gape of mouth, the bewildered eyes and terror. And then—we were alone in the house, with no car—came the scream of sirens, the EMTs leaping down, Grey terrified of the lights, the strangers, the blood, my fear . . . but he's safe, *safe*, my son is safe and in his bed at last, and the new beauty of medical insurance tolls like a soft sweet chime at three AM as I stare at the shining black window and listen to his light breathing in the next room. And I'm living the inescapable wrench in the stomach, the breaths that bring no air, knowing that the difference between that neat black square and the space he'd leave behind is that there would be no edges, no boundaries, no place my hands would not keep reaching out in search of him.

Fitting

When I was young and very much in love, I had an older woman friend. She was a restless writer in her fifties who had grown up in Brazil, worked in Ecuador, and was on her fourth husband; she had a knowing air. We met in a graduate course. Estranged from her own adult daughter, she took an interest in my upcoming wedding, helping me plan, volunteering to make food for the reception, and, in a strange and surprising gesture of generosity, offering to let me wear her own wedding dress.

I had mostly lost my own mother when I'd run away at fourteen, and my young stepmother and I were friendly but not close. This new friend, with her long career in social justice, colorful jewelry, and black leggings, was both glamorous and kind, and I appreciated her attentions. But one day she said casually about my fiancé, "He's never going to set the world on fire."

Today, thinking back, this seems like an unconscionably cruel thing to say to a young person in love. I'm in my forties now, and I cannot imagine myself uttering such words to, for example, one of my young graduate students.

But at the time, I'm ashamed to say, I let myself be troubled by my friend's remark. It hurt me; it gave me doubts about my choice. Later, when I was tactless enough to confide what was bothering me to my fiancé, it hurt him, too.

Reader, he married me anyway. Fifteen years later, we are still very happy.

Now, thinking back, I wonder what led my friend, this older woman, to intervene in such a way. She barely knew my fiancé, after all, aside from brief hellos and the facts that he studied Chaucer and played soccer and guitar. Why did she imagine that her view was a fitting thing to share with me? Was it an attempt to offer the sort of blunt advice for which female friendships are supposedly known? Perhaps it was a desire to draw closer to me by chuckling about men behind their backs: you know, *men*—those hapless, hopeless things. Was it an impulse to protect, to mother me? Perhaps she wanted to warn me against disappointment in marriage, a feeling she presumably knew. Did she feel she had issued fair warning? Beginning to see the roots of her estrangement from her daughter, I recalled the words of my own mother, twice divorced, when, years earlier, I'd shared my happiness over the new boyfriend who later became my son's father.

"Well, enjoy it now," she'd said bitterly. "It won't last."

It hadn't. My own judgment was a thing I couldn't trust.

Whatever motivated my new friend, her words discouraged me. They took a little of the wind out of my sails. But, as with so many moments in my life when a person has said something that shocked or hurt or galled me, I found myself stunned into a pained and confused silence, unable to retort.

What I wish for my younger, blindsided self in her twenties is the capacity to have talked back, to have said this: I don't *want* someone who'll set the world on fire. I hope for someone who'll listen and be kind and be there, someone enthused about all the private domestic delights I cherish, someone interesting and thoughtful and sane. If he should happen to set the world on fire, so be it, but that's not what I'm *after*.

But I couldn't say that at the time, much less claim my own flickering desire to set the world—or at least my little portion of it—on fire all by myself. Perhaps to claim such a desire was even more impossible for my friend, more than a generation older, and that's why it felt crucial to her to hitch oneself to a star—a man who could provide excitement, talent, and naked ambition, a man openly possessed of that drive she so clearly felt herself.

Fifteen years after a ceremony that featured burritos, champagne, a cantina, and a thunderstorm that drenched us all with silver sheets of rain as we rushed in the dark to our cars, neither my husband nor I—I'm relieved to say—has set the world on fire.

Perhaps it's for the best. Poor world, it's been burnt enough.

Instead, we have our own quiet, deeply happy lives, with our small accomplishments and satisfactions, all on a very modest, human scale. I feel sorry that I hurt him, in his twenties, by sharing my friend's casual judgment—that I measured him against a standard I wasn't even sure I shared. I'm sorry that men were and still are made to feel that they must be larger than life and achieve extraordinary things in order to earn love. "Women have served all these centuries," writes Virginia Woolf, "as looking-glasses possessing the magic and delicious power of reflecting the figure of man at twice its natural size. Without that power probably the earth would still be swamp and jungle. The glories of all our wars," she concludes drily, "would be unknown." The ill-fitting roles prescribed by gender have so often warped the truth of human selves. Women, pressed into service as mirrors, rightly resented the duty of flattery, while men, yearning for love, felt pressured to do great and sometimes dastardly deeds.

I wonder if dismissing men for failing to do so was how my friend kept some sacred core of herself safe, aloof, superior.

In her home one sunlit afternoon, she invited me to try on her wedding dress. We entered her walk-in closet and stood in front of her three-way mirror as she hooked me into what she'd worn. Under her kind and interested gaze, I felt honored and also cared for in a way I had long craved. My own mother—the bitter one, the Jehovah's Witness who raised me—wanted nothing to do with me. My biological mother, who'd given me away at birth, had recently appeared in my life, and she was also excited about my wedding, but she, too, wanted me to wear her wedding gown, a gown from a marriage that had collapsed. When she met my older woman friend, I could have sworn a strange, competitive tension crackled in the hot Texas air between them, as if each were vying to step into a long-vacated role.

Their eagerness was kind, but I felt awkward and confused, like a token in a foreign game. I wanted to please my newly met birth-mother, and I wanted to please my older woman friend, but I didn't want to inherit their terms of engagement.

In *A Room of One's Own*, Virginia Woolf describes the conditions a woman needs to be a writer. People generally remember the two most famous ones: a room of her own and five hundred pounds a year (today, about forty thousand dollars) of independent—a discreet way of saying unearned—income. Woolf herself had an inheritance and servants. Well remembered, too, are her repeated references to childlessness, a condition that, by twenty, I had no hope of sharing. But only twice in her book does she mention the desirability of having "the best of husbands." Her own husband, Leonard Woolf, was just such a man, an important political writer who nonetheless made food for her, supported her work, recognized its worth, accepted her romantic relationships with women, and cared for her when she was physically and mentally ill. But his kindness and support get short shrift in *A Room of One's Own*, which had other fish to fry. In my twenties, reading the book in graduate school, I failed to notice Woolf's "best of husbands" references. As I teach it now in my forties, after years with a kind, patient, interesting man, who brings me toast and tea in the mornings, would rather see me write than clean house, loves and supports my son like his own, and doesn't mind when I stay up grading papers late into the night, they seem writ large.

On that afternoon so many years ago in the air-conditioned closet of my friend's bedroom, encased in the pale lace of her dress, my reflection looked pretty enough, but I still remember the feeling as I turned from side to side in her mirror: clammy, caged, wrong. She said the gown fit perfectly, and I hesitated in the late sun and the warmth of her interest, unsure of what to do.

After the wedding, my friend and I fell slowly out of touch. I finished my PhD and left town for my first job, while she divorced and moved to a different state. The last I heard, she had married again.

That day in the carpeted hush of her closet, I declined her kind offer. Later I declined my birthmother's, too. I bought my own dress with my own earned money and walked alone down the plush, red aisle to where the best of husbands waited, radiant.

And reader: I looked pretty good.

The Athens of the Midwest

The town where I live has exactly three attractions. One of them's a jail.

It's a town of fifteen thousand in rural Indiana, the flat, unpictur-esque part. Most of the adults in our neighborhood work in one of the sixteen factories that keep the place alive. Our next-door neigh-bor Laura handles financial aid at the college where I work; her hus-band works the eleven-to-seven shift bonding sheets of paper into slabs that become brake pads at the Raybestos plant half a mile from our houses. At night, when the day-noises of traffic, trains, birds, and kids die down, we hear its hum through our dark bedroom window. Our town has the highest divorce rate in Indiana—due to all the shift work, people say.

All of the attractions are about a hundred years old, from the time when the town called itself—proudly, hopefully—the Athens of the Midwest. There's the Lane Place, the preserved historic home of Henry Lane, once a governor, once a congressman, the chairman of the first Republican National Convention. Its grounds, a full city block, are green and shady; the house is large and white, with white columns and green shutters. Inside are what you'd expect, old furniture and rugs and silverware from the original estate, and across the drive is a log cabin that was moved to the site. It might have been a stop on the Underground Railroad, the sign tells us. Rough-made and small and brown, its satiny old walls are a relief after walking through so many things you can't touch.

There's a gazebo, built just a few years ago, on the grounds. Our first Thanksgiving here, when my brother Tony visited us, we took sandwiches there, goofed around, lured squirrels with our crusts. Yellow-leafed gingko trees dropped sticky fruits that smelled like dogshit, and we threw them at each other. But the president of the college—which is to say, my boss—and his wife live in the comparably huge and historic white house immediately across the street: the Elston Place, with its metal sign explaining the history and accomplishments of the Elston family. I felt a little inhibited.

Walking distance from the Lane Place, as almost everything is, lies the Ben Hur Museum, also known as the Lew Wallace Study, a beautiful and bizarre architectural tribute to Lew Wallace by Lew Wallace, paid for by the proceeds from *Ben Hur*, the bestselling novel of the nineteenth century, which outsold every book except the Bible—and that was even before the Broadway production was mounted in 1899, with real chariots, eight real horses, and real dust.

The three-and-a-half-acre plot of the Lew Wallace Study is enclosed by brick walls too high to see over, and the study itself, a mix of Byzantine, Greek, and Roman architecture, has walls a foot and a half thick made of vitrified brick brought in from Akron, Ohio, and a steel floor with Carnegie beams. In the 1890s, it cost thirty thousand dollars. Suddenly, asking my son Grey and his friend to take their conversation out of the kitchen, where I write at the table between meals, seems vastly less Frank-Lloyd-Wrightish than it had.

"I want a study, a pleasure-house for my soul, where no one could hear me make speeches to myself, and play the violin at midnight if

I chose," Lew wrote to his wife, Susan Elston (yes) Wallace, in 1879. The building's odd domed roof has oxidized to whitish green; the reflecting pool and stocked moat where Lew once fished with his grandson are now filled in and covered by grass. The guides can show you approximately where Lew's horse Old John was buried near the south wall, but they can't be sure about the precise spot. They seem apologetic.

The interior is filled with felicities from foreign lands: stone cannonballs from the Battle of Constantinople, an alabaster urn on a green onyx pedestal, a stone marker inscribed with Greek from a Roman catacomb. General Wallace governed the New Mexico Territory and was even, for four years, the minister to Turkey. Susan went along, writing five books about his diplomatic postings: *The Land of the Pueblos*, *Along the Bosphorus*, *The Storied Sea*. What was it like for a woman in the 1880s to travel to Jerusalem, London, Mexico? Particularly a woman born and raised in the creamiest family in a provincial town of fifteen thousand (as it was even then, in its heyday). But her books, out of print, are housed under glass.

The spiral staircase curves down sharply, and the steps are narrow and steep. My whole foot won't fit onto any of them. In the basement, the padlocked doors of a storage room gape a little: you can see the carriage Lew brought back from Paris, specially made. Castor oil, instead of the usual tar, lubricated its bearings. The great-great-grandfather of a boy in Grey's class used to drive him.

Little moves here. Little changes. People stay. The things that happened last year happen again. Grey's friends' parents down the block were high school sweethearts; now divorced, they live in houses on opposite sides of the street. Our next-door neighbors detasseled corn together in high school during the summers. Grey agitates for daytrips to Lafayette or Indianapolis every weekend.

The Old Jail Museum, our third thing to write home about, was a wonder in its time. One of only seven of its kind ever built in the world, it contains within its Victorian brick façade a barred revolving cylinder two stories high. Each level is split into eight pie-slice-shaped cells, and the lines between the wedges are solid metal sheets, to keep the prisoners from seeing or touching each other, while the outer edge of each cell is barred, with a barred door. In this way, only one prisoner at a time from each level could exit his cell on the landing. Guards could walk all around, seeing everything at all times: sort of a panopticon in reverse, with the prisoners in the central tower. The whole contraption can be turned by a giant handcrank so smooth and well designed that a strong child can move the rooms of thirty-two men.

Heavy gray paint coats everything. I stepped into the cell, its smallness, its sterility, the quaver of its mobile floor, and felt suddenly unsteady and sick, as if I were breathing misery. I left after only a moment, though the fascinated couple behind me stayed. The man jumped up and down, testing for something I didn't hear.

Tenure, it strikes me sometimes, is a strange thing to want. Lifetime employment—lifetime anything. My little brother's a mechanic in Texas. Our father saw going to college as a luxury, something superfluous, something other people did. In our family, I was the first. And now the possibility of reading and writing for the rest of my life shimmers just ahead like a mirage, the possibility of actually spending my days as someone who paces in her black loafers up and down a classroom where Ezra Pound once taught.

But forever in a small town's a long time. My friends in Manhattan, in San Francisco, email me jokes about the fly-over, ask how the corn's growing. An East Coast friend—who sees it as his obligation *as a writer* to attend every art opening, every new play—sent a thank-you card after a recent visit: "It's nice to spend time with someone who seems to appreciate what she's got," it said. I reread it, wondering if envy or pity was what he felt.

There were things we weren't prepared for. Two nights after we moved ourselves in on a hundred-degree August day, I was sent to

Blockbuster by an exhausted husband. My wallet flapped open on the counter as I pulled out credit cards and my Texas driver's license to support my freshly inked-in application. The clerk—tall, young, with short sandy hair and a stack of twine-and-bead necklaces—looked me up and down. "Hey," he finally said, "are you a new professor up at the college?"

"Yes," I said, startled that he'd recognized my new ID card from just its visible edge. I ran my hands quickly through my hair and tried, without looking down, to remember what clothes I had on.

"What department?" he asked, and I told him; it turned out that he was majoring in English himself.

"So, whatcha got here?" he asked, picking up my plastic choice, and I quailed for a moment, recalling how I'd lingered in the aisle in front of *Kama Sutra*, wondering if we even had the energy for anything it might inspire—but no, I'd chosen Kenneth Branagh's *Hamlet*. I breathed again. The student was suitably impressed: even begrimed, sweaty professors, it seemed, professors not yet thirty, unwound with Culture.

Two friends of ours, untenured professors having an affair, leave town to eat out.

The Kroger is a hotbed of chance encounters. Once we counted six faculty and seven students in twenty aisles. I stopped wearing my Grateful Dead t-shirt to run errands; I began wearing makeup on weekends. I covertly checked my husband for little stains and holes.

When I had a driving accident the summer of our second year here, it made front-page news—the other headline read, "Horse Gives Rare Birth to Twins." A photograph shot from street level made our little white Honda loom large and wicked, a killer. Two people from work had passed the accident (in front of the courthouse, during the noon hour) and returned to campus bearing the news that I was probably dead. Our phone rang all day.

Secrets are hard to keep here. All traffic violations, for example, are announced on the radio each morning. In this fashion, it became a matter for great mirth in our building that a colleague in philosophy, known for her gentle and deliberate manner, had recklessly not come to a complete stop at a stop sign.

"The town where I grew up was so dull," my father liked to joke, speaking of Key West, "that for excitement we used to go downtown and watch the parking meters violate themselves." Here the meters give us half an hour for a nickel, an hour for a dime. Their black slots aren't tall enough for quarters. If you should find a ticket tucked under your wiper in a bright yellow envelope, you need only enclose fifty cents, seal the envelope, and drop it one of the red metal boxes that dot the streets. On Saturdays and Sundays, all the meters wear blue plastic hoods that thank us for shopping downtown.

Sometimes I walk the streets in the evening with Grey and James, coming out of the China Inn or Little Mexico, or with just James, strolling up and down the block outside The Olde Paint Store, waiting for Grey to finish his Thursday-night drawing class. The brick fronts of the buildings are crisped in black shadow, and their roofs cut a knife-edge across a sky such a brilliant blue, a perfect cyan darkening as it rises, that it stops my breath. Maxfield Parrish put this sky behind his snowy houses, his scarf-draped girls. Around us are the little shops, the restaurants without signs open only for lunch, the gold stone courthouse like a set from a John Grisham movie, the sky with its visible stars.

Just off the main road north out of town lies what used to be the old warehouse district. The red brick buildings, three and five stories tall (taller than the downtown), used to be the end of the line, the last signs of life before you left.

Now things have developed, a little. If you drive north through a couple miles of greenery, you'll bump into the anonymous little civilization that sprang up when the interstate went through: the Holiday Inn, the McDonald's, the forgettable housing development, the Burger King, some convenience stores, a strip club, a new Comfort Inn opened by the Indian American family of a girl in Grey's class. The new road they broke through a crop field is called Gandhi Street. Behind the hotel, Guaravi's parents have planted a vegetable garden. I've seen them out there holding hands, looking down at what's growing.

But from downtown, the warehouse district still looks like the end of the line before the road north swerves and dips into trees. I walk there sometimes, thinking: If these beautiful old buildings, this district, these brick roads, were in some city (Portland, Maine; Austin, Texas; your town, maybe), developers would pounce. In no time, there would be strings of tiny white lights roping the trees, the plate-glass windows, the newly installed French doors, which would open into coffee shops with actual cappuccino, and little clubs with live music on the weekends, and restaurants that people would call bistros and cafés with salads they would call exquisite. There would be couples strolling after dark, women catching their heels in the bricks. The city would put in period streetlamps to enhance the area's historic charm, and the buildings' upper levels would be rented by hip singles and couples. There would be a bakery that sold orange-cranberry bread and lemon-poppyseed bread and all the other breads you can't buy fresh in town. Pumpernickel, sourdough. Our local Lexuses and suvs and three new Volkswagen Beetles would park diagonally with their noses close to the brick.

But the buildings mostly stand empty. Ivy covers the town's name on the side of one: "dsville Seed Co.," it reads. Another has a sign, "Indiana Farm Bureau Co-op Seed House," but through its pocked windows honeycombed with wire, there are only rolls of carpet and carpet padding, flopped haphazardly on the concrete floor. A rough expanse of sandy bulldozed dirt gives onto the best view in town: the semblance of hills, covered lushly with dark green trees, tinting blue from the atmosphere. It's the same view I used to stare at from my table at the Java Roaster downtown before it folded, pretending I was in Colorado.

The one building that's alive is Magic Light Neon. I don't know who buys neon here; no new neon signs have gone up since we moved to town three years ago. But the studio seems to be flourishing. At the turn of each holiday, a new neon sign appears on the rooftop: a shamrock-laden red-haired guy, red and blue fireworks, a ghost, Santa Claus with his arm waving jerkily between three positions. When we're driving home tired at night from Lafayette or Chicago or Milwaukee, it's like a welcome sign, a hokey beacon that promises, "Just five minutes now."

When we moved in, the owners nearly forgot to leave us the keys. "Well, you won't need them anyway," they said. They never locked their doors. People leave their car windows rolled down for the breeze. When Laura and her family go away for the weekend, Grey takes care of their brown dog Babe. "Just use the back door," they say. "It's always open."

After living in New Orleans and San Antonio, not hermetically sealing the house was strange. But we're adjusting. Our downstairs windows stay open all night: the house, which has no air-conditioning, wakes up cool. When our arthritic golden lab, emboldened by age, escapes the yard for a jaunt, all the neighbor kids know whose she is and vie to bring her back. The front door lock, original from the 1890s, broke off last year. We have not replaced it.

When I was seven, my mother would send me to the Utotem for milk. I'd carry it back in my flowered plastic bike basket, feeling independent, a citizen of the world. But Miami stopped being the place it had been. Big kids threw rocks at grade-schoolers. Gangs formed; people got shot. Sex crimes were on TV. My parents moved us north in a Ryder truck to West Virginia, where houses were cheap, and we lived in safe boring towns that I ached to get out of, where diners like the Poky-Dot had condensed jukeboxes at each table playing only country, and real places had names like Sally's Motel and Bait Shop. "Sleep here and get worms," my brother and I would hoot out the window, laughing helplessly, every time we passed. I sketched urban skylines in the margins of my homework and counted the years to graduation.

Sometimes our son calls this a nowhere town. He walks with his friend to the shop that sells baseball cards, and they walk home. He rides his bike miles to the public pool, swims all afternoon with his friends, and bikes back without incident. Without gates and guards, without security cars roving neighborhoods built to seem like neighborhoods once were, he moves in the kind of safety and freedom my father remembered from his boyhood in Key West in the 1940s. "It's boring here," Grey says.

He's only in seventh grade, but he knows already that he wants to go to Oberlin, major in Asian studies, live in Tokyo. Tokyo, I think. I've seen the hotels where businessmen sleep in little cubicles like body drawers at a morgue, the streets where a thousand signs litter the air. I've tutored Japanese students: "Even on vacation, we stay with crowds. We never like to be alone."

Sometimes after work and school, we drive twenty minutes to Shades, the state park, and are the only people there. We park in the silent lot and walk through the darkening forest. Far below the lookout, Sugar Creek gleams in the dusk. A raccoon lumbers across the shallows to an island. He's a speck. Leaves shiver and glint, blanketing the hills in all directions.

When we drive away, it's dark. Fireflies rise glowing from a field of soy. In the distance, a buck and three does raise their heads. We stop the car; no one's behind us. The fireflies lift from the dark leaves in layers of glimmering green, twinkling like a foreign city, like the lights of a runway at night, welcoming you down to the strange new place where you've landed.

You Can Avoid the Mistakes I Made

There's a way you can tell when people are serious about killing themselves: they look kind of funny around the gills, like they're breathing harder, faster, just to get enough air. Their eyes wander, dull like the eyes of old dogs, gloss lost, brown marbles gone sticky and coated with dust, staring off to a place you can't see. When they laugh, their hands tremble, and they laugh when nothing's funny, a high cracked sound like the squawk of a grackle spearing the air. In the shower, water puddles around their feet, clinging near them with a new molecular gravity as if reluctant to let them go, and when they lift their feet there's a weird sucking sound, a wet dirge, as the water rushes into the damp foot-shaped spaces on the tile, obliterates each trace of them.

There are these signs, but no one tells you, and the little brochures from Health and Human Services come too late.

My father is a dead man now, and the space where he used to be is a corridor of ruined Sundays, a bakery of stale cakes fallen in at their centers.

But you have to eat, so you eat, and everything crumbles dry in your mouth, tasteless. Sundays keep coming, and you leave the phone in its electric black cradle where it does not ring, where the sacred numbers will not appear again in the little screen. The kindly people don't ask anymore, and you are assumed to be over it all, and you assume that, too. Except when the spasms come over you and you put your hand out to the wall and wait. Wait. And then you do resume breathing, and eventually you resign yourself to that as well.

And nothing's happening in the plot of after-the-suicide, no one's going anywhere or doing anything or having interesting conflicts that might soon be resolved in some unexpected yet believable fashion. There's just an emptiness where a story's supposed to be, and that's how it is, that's how it feels, that's how death leaves you when they kill themselves.

An Angle of Vision

As formerly poor women now working as writers in and out of the academy, the gifts we bring—not only to the readers of our work but also to the institutions that currently shelter us—are an angle of vision and the will for change.

When I took my first teaching job, I was startled by all the food. Everywhere, food—good food, free for the taking. At department meetings, the chair would lay out a spread: crackers, grapes, cheese, expensive little cookies. At division meetings: a similar spread, with wine. At lunchtime talks, no one brought brown bags; dozens of pizza boxes stood stacked on the table outside, and students helped themselves. After evening lectures and readings, there were always receptions with cookies, hors d'oeuvres, piles of cut fresh fruit, washed strawberries—even, sometimes, tapas. There were permanent lines in the budget for these things.

This astonished me. For the first time in my life, at twenty-nine, I was earning a salary that put me above the minimum wage; I could buy all the food I wanted with my own money. Yet here was this perpetual buffet, free, for people who did not need it.

It was not the first time academia has amazed me. As a sixteen-year-old heading across the country, a first-generation college student at a country-club college, I didn't know a lot of things. I didn't know how to play tennis or how to ski. Carless, fresh from factory work, I didn't know that kids my age drove their parents' hand-me-down Volvos and convertible Mercedes. I didn't know the words *paradigm* or *paradox* or *essentialism*. When at seventeen I dropped out, I didn't know I was just another at-risk retention statistic; that domestic violence rates leap by a factor of five when families live below the poverty line, as ours had; or that children in low-income homes are raised in ways that render higher education and professional achievement difficult because of deep attitudes parents convey about one's worth and the right to speak up. And I didn't know that the word *testimony* could mean something besides the scary, throat-pounding experiences I'd had in courtrooms, lawyers' offices, and judges' chambers. Testifying didn't feel like power, though it and the cops did get my brother removed from the abusive and poverty-stricken home I'd run away from. It didn't feel like power. It felt like terror, like telling, like telling on my own mother, like lifting up the veil on the violence and hunger and pathology she'd tried so hard to hide, a veil that schoolteachers and classmates and even the other Jehovah's Witnesses were content to leave hanging there, even after they knew. That veil of poverty and dysfunction hung there like a vertical safety net, keeping them comfortably on their side, while we and the trauma we suffered were effectively invisible.

"You save yourself or you remain unsaved," I read in *Lucky*, Alice Sebold's memoir, as I prepared to teach it in a senior seminar for English majors at that college, where I later earned tenure, where I chaired my department from a corner office with windows and a beautiful rug.

You get used to things. I taught at my first institution for ten years, and I called catering to order fine dinners for our visiting poets, our job candidates, our senior English majors, and I signed the invoices when they were sent to me. It was no longer jarring or strange.

So it is easy for me to empathize with my colleagues and students. If I, who have known hunger and food stamps, dry pancakes for dinner for nights on end, who stole food as a hungry child—if I can grow accustomed to plenty, if what once astonished me can become routine, then I can understand the obliviousness of my colleagues who have never known want.

The flaunting of privilege and the connections privilege draws among gender, race, and class are not new. In the Europe of the 1200s, only the head of the household could urinate in the great hall, where people dined, his phallus a marvelously literal, visible signifier of privilege. Centuries later, such manifestations of linked privileges are much rarer, and those that remain are subtler.

But at my former institution, where my office trash disappeared in the night, emptied by the hands of a woman I never saw, the nexus of class and gender privilege remains writ unusually large: Wabash College is one of the last three remaining all-male private liberal arts colleges in the country. "Why do women like Wabash men?" asked the front of the red t-shirt of a student in my intro creative writing class. In a pun that explicitly links masculinity to institutional wealth, the back of the t-shirt read, "Because we're well endowed." And they are: Wabash has a 370-million-dollar endowment for an enrollment of 850 young men—per student, it's one of the highest endowments in the country, and the institution remains adamantly all-male. "Co-Ed Never," reads another t-shirt. All of the trustees are men, and most are white; one described board membership as "the most exclusive men's club in Indiana." Wabash's president, dean, CFO, and deans of advancement, admissions, and student life were all white men when I left, and white men comprised 74 percent of the faculty. The thick crimson carpet that unspooled across the wooden floor of my historic building, thicker than the carpeting of any home I've lived in, was vacuumed each night by invisible women and then tromped on each day by hundreds of young men.

For a woman coming from an impoverished background, a woman who took the first job offered in a tough market, it was a very strange environment, a place where the intersections of male privilege and class privilege were constantly foregrounded, where my own twinned vulnerabilities of poverty and femaleness were repeatedly drawn to my attention.

For several years, I struggled to pass as a native, fell silent when I had no cultural capital to contribute to the conversation, which was most of the time. People called me shy, and I thought of myself that way. But I wasn't. Rather, I was incognito, unknowable—strategically so, and it was a strategy born of shame and desperation, of the felt sense that who I really was would disturb people too much to let me stay. I was a stranger in a strange land, a trailer-trash girl from a fucked-up background whose test scores and polite smile and diligence let her slip inoffensively upward.

The classroom was fine, a space of clearly delineated topics, a conversation I could prepare for. So I prepared, and prepared, with the same determination that had gotten me through my junior year of college, twenty, nursing a new baby, living in a sketchy barrio on WIC and food stamps, getting straight As. That kind of doggedness, I brought to my preps, my grading, my articles about leftist-feminist writers, the experimental short fiction I published about Latina waitresses, housecleaners, minimum-wage shopgirls.

But there was no way to prepare for the other part of academic life at my institution, the part that, as a grad student, I had been spared: the dinner parties, receptions, and cocktail hours, the social life where people chatted off the grid—and, weirdly, as I soon learned, not about ideas at all, as I had always fondly imagined, but about vacation plans and good restaurants and cultural activities and *So, where did you grow up?* With massive student loans to pay, my vacations were staying home with my son and husband, and our restaurants of choice were Taco Bell and Subway. My discretionary income and spare time went to the "cultural activity" of therapy, where I was still working through the symptoms of post-traumatic stress disorder.

Where I grew up, and how, and that I ran away at fourteen—those were off-limits. Everything true about my background was shocking, vulgar, fodder for tabloids: abuse, rootlessness, broken families, weird religion, prison. I didn't want to seem unseemly, didn't want anyone's pity, didn't want to scare or repel anyone with the monstrous background I carried, the monstrous anxieties that still plagued me. I certainly did not "authorize [my] desire," as Emma Pérez writes in *The Decolonial Imaginary*, "through third space feminist practice by deliberately fashioning a sexed body for public consumption." Instead, I deliberately fashioned a sexless, undistracting body for classroom and committee-meeting consumption.

The tenure track in a small community is a tightrope. I worked hard to reveal nothing, not to fall, to just keep placing one foot in front of the other, eyes on the prize of tenure and tuition remission for my son.

I was entering my fifth year of college teaching before I learned that all my departmental colleagues had a woman.

For four years, I'd wondered in frustration and despair how my colleagues were able to entertain so freely, their houses immaculate when we arrived, while our own hundred-year-old, un-air-conditioned, badly heated house—with a growing son and a blond collie-lab mix who lived indoors—was always considerably more chaotic. Each weeknight, I worked late after dinner, grading and preparing for class, and my husband worked full-time, so the laundry, cleaning, and yardwork were left until the weekends. I was exhausted, my husband was exhausted, and the house was still a mess, unfit for throwing the dinner parties that were a staple of social life in our small town. We did manage to host a couple of dinners, but they left me drained, not glowing. Old feelings from childhood flared up: I felt ashamed of my family's dirtiness and guilty that I couldn't work hard enough to fix it.

Oh, yes, my older male colleagues told me on the ride to the state park where our annual retreat was held, they all had women who came in. Their wives all worked, so they all had women who came in once a week or oftener to clean.

For me, it was a light bulb, a paradigm shift. My colleagues weren't cleaner, purer, more scrupulous people by nature. They hired help.

I felt queasy at the prospect, though. When I was growing up, my mother cleaned houses; so did my aunt. My relations were the women people had. To now be a person who hired such a woman put me on the wrong side of the equation, away from what felt familiar, safe, and comfortable.

My husband and I tried, but it felt weird, and a housecleaner was an expense we ultimately found we could not afford. We gave up. Our house went back to being lower-class messy, and we failed to reciprocate the generous invitations we received.

Jumping class comes at a price, and the price is not belonging. Within academia and the publishing world, I often find myself occupying a space of painful ambiguity. I don't fit, don't know the rules— didn't know until this year, for example, that you're supposed to send your agent a gift when he or she lands a book deal for you. (Who knew? Where I come from, people don't get presents for doing their jobs.) So I trip up, make mistakes. In this ambiguous space of not belonging, I waver between shame and guilt, my alliances unclear.

Once I went to dinner with two editors who were publishing my work. They were nice women, I liked them, and I was excited to be in a big city trying sushi for the first time. Over dinner, talk turned to the professions of our cousins. (Siblings are boring, said one editor; everyone talks about their siblings.) The two women's cousins were art gallery owners and attorneys and things I can't remember now, and then it was my turn. At the time, I wasn't in close touch with my extended family, but I offered what I knew.

"My girl cousins are all secretaries," I said, "and my guy cousins are either cops or the guys who drive the wrecking trucks around after cops."

Both women burst into laughter.

"Oh, you've got to use that!" said one. "It's absolutely priceless." They kept repeating what I'd said and breaking into gales of laughter.

I felt weird: confused and embarrassed—but yeah, okay, I could see how it was funny. I smiled along gamely, feeling ashamed for my cousins, who surely did not know, as I had not, that their hardworking lives were a matter for mirth.

My brother, a mechanic, had no such ambivalence. When I later confided my confusion and discomfort about the incident, he didn't hesitate.

"Well, fuck you very much," he said, as if addressing the two editors directly. "I'm glad you find our family so *funny*. I'm glad we could *amuse* you."

My brother's clarity is undimmed, his allegiance clear; he stands on solid ground. His friends work construction and renovation. They and their wives are smart, kind, and interesting. But they drink beer and smoke cigarettes around their toddlers, which makes me uneasy, and sometimes their humor concerns bodily functions. Forcing weak smiles about anal leakage, I feel uptight, a snob.

I love my brother and his wife, and I really like the people in their circle, but I don't fit there, even when I sit around their campfire drinking beer. I don't fit anywhere.

For me as a writer, each choice to disclose true information comes with the anxiety of betrayal, whether I reveal things about my poor family, whom I love, or the rich institution that sheltered me, where many people were kind and generous.

"Oh, you've got to use that!" laughed the editor. And now I have.

Happy to be a visiting writer at Vanderbilt University, where one can safely hazard that the majority of students do not come from backgrounds of poverty or working-class labor, I opened my reading by holding up a water glass from the cushy Nashville hotel where the university was housing me.

I don't drink out of such glasses, I said, and neither should they. I'd recently seen on TV a hidden-camera exposé of hotel maids using toxic chemical cleaners to wipe out the glasses and then setting them back on the counters, unwashed, and putting the little covers on them to indicate that they were clean. The TV voiceover remarked in horror on the practice. Were the maids stupid? The camera zoomed close to the large-lettered warnings on the bottles full of blue liquid. Could they not read?

I don't think it's either one. For sure, those women don't squirt Windex on the glasses from which their children drink at home.

It's not ignorance. It's not illiteracy.

"No," I told the Vanderbilt audience. "That's class rage."

For formerly poor women in the academy and publishing, our challenge is how not to let our rage become toxic, how to use it to clean things up for real.

At my own institution, it was strange to be so frequently the only one in a committee meeting arguing for my point of view. In my first year on the Visiting Artists Series Committee, for example, I couldn't understand why we charged local citizens for events with big-name visiting artists when our budget covered all the costs. The committee chair voiced the committee's traditional argument for charging local citizens fifteen and twenty dollars a ticket: that people wouldn't *appreciate* the arts if they didn't *pay* for them. The rest of the (all-male) committee smiled patiently as I tried to explain a position that had never before been voiced at that table: If someone has never *been* to a ballet or a live theater performance, how will he or she *know* to appreciate it?

It took some doing, but our old policy did change. Wabash's auditoriums are now regularly packed, and our sharing of the arts with the larger community resulted in better town-gown relations. Looking back now, everyone agrees we made the right choice.

And we made the right choice to fund and teach in Indiana's first Clemente Course, which offers a college-level curriculum free to poor people. It was the right choice, when I took students to England for a fully funded study trip, to invite as chaperone not another faculty member, as was customary, but our department secretary; and it was the right choice to offer free creative writing workshops through the public library and at the domestic violence shelter.

As women coming from the condition of poverty, we bring an immediacy, an urgency to the table. We cannot falsely imagine that, because our suffering has ended, it does not go on and on. As accustomed as we might become to the presence of sufficient food, we cannot forget, as Toni Morrison writes, that "the function of freedom is to free someone else."

Friends had urged me to write a memoir, but I couldn't. I knew the market was glutted. I couldn't bear to open those wounds, that shame, the terror, only to have my tale trounced by reviewers sick of sob stories, of writers they called narcissistic, attention-seeking. Attention was a thing I didn't want.

But my silence about my background ended when, the summer before my tenure year, my father shot himself. It was too big to conceal. The dirt. The drama.

My memoir appeared in 2005: *The Truth Book*, titled with deliberate irony after the book used with new converts by Jehovah's Witnesses, the religion I'd been adopted into at birth, a complicated religion that practiced racial and ethnic equality, which my assimilating Latino father hungered for; a religion that prohibited any desire for material objects—that forbade, at that time, going to college; a religion predicated on severe gender hierarchy, so that it was a mark of godliness for a woman to be silent and submissive, as I was raised to be; a religion that preached ignorance of the body, that children were to be immediately obedient to adults in all things, that men were the unquestionable heads of the household, and that sexual molestation was only actionable if it had been witnessed by two neutral adult observers; an evangelical Christian sect that has historically appealed to the poor and working class by promising us beautiful houses on a paradise earth, as soon as the apocalypse wipes away all the worldly people.

The thought of having this book—the story of my trashy, messed-up life, my hurt young female body—available to my middle-class, mostly male, mostly white, often quite privileged colleagues and students was unnerving.

My son, who's now nineteen, a college junior, has not read my book. A wise child with good boundaries, he says he knows it would make him sad. He wants to keep intact his image of me as the mama he has always known: his protector, brave, in charge.

My students and colleagues felt, of course, no such compunction, and I had to confront the fact that many of them—and I might never know which—would see me in that other, vulnerable way: young and poor, living in trashy places and wearing the clothes kids ridicule, and violated in body and spirit. Weird. Visible.

To write my book, I had to reinhabit, without shame, that place of shame, of trauma, of anguish and silence. I had to give it a voice.

To put my art into the world as memoir, I had to be willing to stand as the living, visible representative of the text, the body at the front of the room.

To be a writer is to claim a voice, a hard thing for anyone schooled to silence. To publish autobiographical work is to be the word made flesh in front of audience after audience, formal when you tour and informal when you return home to your community, which views you with new eyes. You, who have suffered so from being the helpless object of the male gaze, the inadequate object of the classed gaze— "You live *there*?"—you step deliberately now into the spotlight, your scars as visible as your competence. You step into the light on your own terms now, you claim the mic, telling the story you have come here to tell.

Grip

Over the crib in the tiny apartment, there hung a bullet-holed paper target, the size and dark shape of a man, its heart zone, head zone, perforated where my aim had torn through: thirty-six little rips, no strays, centered on spots that would make a man die.

Beginner's luck, said the guys at the shooting range, at first. *Little lady*, they'd said, until the silhouette slid back and farther back. They'd cleared their throats, fallen silent.

A bad neighborhood. An infant child. A Ruger GP .357 with speed-loader.

It's not as morbid as it sounds, a target pinned above a crib: the place was small, the walls already plastered full with paintings, sketches, pretty leaves, hand-illuminated psychedelic broadsides of poems by my friends. I masking-taped my paper massacre to the only empty space, a door I'd closed to form a wall.

When my stepfather got out of prison, he tracked my mother down.

He found the city where she'd moved. He broke a basement window and crawled in. She never saw his car, halfway up the dark block, stuffed behind a bush.

My mother lived. She wouldn't say what happened in the house that night. Cops came: that's what I know. Silent, she hung a screen between that scene and me. It's what a mother does.

She lived—as lived the violence of our years with him, knifed into us like scrimshaw cut in living bone.

Carved but alive, we learned to hold our breath, dive deep, bare our teeth to what fed us.

When I was twenty-one, my son slept under the outline of what I could do, a death I could hold in my hands.

At the time, I'd have denied its locale any meaning, called its placement coincidence, pointing to walls crowded with other kinds of dreams.

But that dark torn thing did hang there, its lower edge obscured behind the wooden slats, the flannel duck, the stuffed white bear.

It hung there like a promise, like a headboard, like a *No*, like a terrible poem, like these lines I will never show you, shielding you from the fear I carry—like a sort of oath I swore over your quiet sleep.

Getting "Grip"

Upon accepting the previous piece, "Grip," for publication in the journal *Fourth Genre*, the editor kindly invited me to write a second essay, explaining its composition. Here, I've tried to do so.

When I finished my memoir *The Truth Book*, I thought I was done with life-writing. I looked forward to returning to fiction and poetry, the genres in which I had trained. *The Truth Book* was harrowing: to draft, to revise—even to read from when I toured. I would return to my hotel rooms exhausted and febrile, trembling, drinking Airborne like a toddy in town after town. When the book's launch was over, I felt relief. I'd gone public with all that awful old material I'd secretly carried (child abuse, fundamentalism, adoption, confusion about my *latinidad*, prison, suicide), and I could let it rest.

I was done drawing on my life for material. *Good-bye to all that.*

So "Grip" came as a surprise.

GENRE

"Grip" came as a poem, initially—a free-verse poem all in one long stanza that obsessed over its central remembered image: the dark, torn paper target hanging over the baby's sweet crib, the contrast of which struck me as strange and compelling in a way it had not when I'd hung the target there myself many years and many dwellings ago.

I can't remember now whether I originally wrote the poem long-hand—which is likely, because that's how I draft almost everything, including this essay—or on my computer in my office, which is where I tinkered with the piece between classes and committee meetings, reading it aloud to myself, gradually seeing that it wanted to break into stanzas. White space helped mark the temporal and topical shifts.

Eventually, the lineation seemed to want to fall away. As a reader, I always wonder if a free-verse poem needs to be a poem. Sometimes the line-breaks do seem important, but sometimes they don't. In the case of "Grip," they didn't. So I let them go, and the piece melted into paragraphs that were indented where the stanzas had begun.

"Grip" came to make more aesthetic sense to me as a very short essay that cares a lot about sound—repetition, rhythm, rhyme—than as a poem.

AUDIENCE

I am usually very unsure about my work—about whether the material that surprises or moves me will matter to anyone else—and it was so with this essay, too.

During the time I was composing it, I was obliged to give a reading every six months at the Pine Manor College MFA program, where I teach. Since most of the faculty and students are there each time, you always have to read something new (or else look washed up). I tried "Grip" out on the audience, and they were very enthusiastic. I was lucky: the audience included poet and editor Steven Huff, who later read "Grip" aloud on his radio show, and the poets Meg Kearney and Laure-Anne Bosselaar, who said kind things about it, and Mike Steinberg, a founding editor of *Fourth Genre*.

Their enthusiastic reception encouraged me to try submitting it. The audience can be very important. It's such a reciprocal relationship.

My real audience, though, is young mothers from backgrounds of poverty and violence, women desperate like the woman I was. I hope "Grip" reaches them.

SUBMERGED

When I submitted "Grip" to *Fourth Genre*, it did not include paragraphs six through eight ("My mother lived . . ."). There was a leap, a gap, and it sounded almost as though my mother could have been dead. She wasn't, but I sort of liked the drama and the absence of certainty.

The editor at *Fourth Genre*, Marcia Aldrich, suggested some changes: "The unanswered question as to your mother's fate is troubling, and a bit more on the roots of the fear that motivates the need to protect your son was identified in our readers' reports. Speaking for myself, I wanted a bit more grounding, or a slight nod in that direction." This seemed like a simple request for fair play with the reader, so I expanded the essay to address those concerns. I added the clarifying material: my mother lived. I agreed with the request for changes, which made it a stronger, fuller piece.

However, I wanted to make sure the essay still said that you could survive something and yet not be alive in quite the same way you were before. To convey something about the way violence can catalyze a kind of poetry of action—not does; *can*—I got the idea of "scrimshaw cut in living bone," which expressed, I thought, an untenable violation that nonetheless might produce a desperate sort of beauty (like hanging a target over a crib). Then I got carried away with literalizing the scrimshaw notion and felt obliged to include the whole whale—an actual whale, swimming about the paragraph. I ran a revised version past my friend and colleague James Engelhardt, a poet and the managing editor at *Prairie Schooner*, who kindly suggested that my inclusion might be a bit over the top, and he was right. It was too abrupt: the reader is first in my old apartment and then at the shooting range, and then sees my mother get attacked, only to be dragged to the depths by a whale that's only metaphorical anyway. Ugh.

So I cut the whale but kept the scrimshaw line, which was all I'd really wanted, and a couple of other phrases that were salvageable: "we learned to hold our breath, dive deep, bare our teeth to what fed us."

In this way, the whale is there yet not there, and posterity will be relieved to find no krill in the piece.

SYNECDOCHE

My stepfather's sexual abuse of me has caused long-lasting damage, but I didn't want to go into all that in "Grip." I'd hashed through it in *The Truth Book*, and I thought that bringing such an explosive topic into so short an essay could derail the piece.

But while I tried to squelch it, it was there for me, psychically, as I was writing. I kept telling it, *This isn't about you: it's about my mom, and my son*, but it wouldn't let itself be silenced. So I compromised with it: I looked for a concrete, true detail that would let me allude to it, which I found in this image of the target: "But that dark torn thing did hang there, its lower edge obscured behind the wooden slats, the flannel duck, the stuffed white bear." That hidden lower edge of the outline—hidden behind the crib slats, hidden in the essay—stood in for my stepfather's abusive sexuality. It functioned as a synecdoche for all of it, the part standing in for the whole.

My psyche accepted that line as a reasonable compromise, a sufficient acknowledgment of that issue, and left me in peace.

The reader doesn't need to know.

TITLE

The title "Grip" was simply a gift. It just came, early on, very soon after the initial poem was down on the page, and although it isn't a word that occurs in the body of the text, it seemed right: my grip on the gun, the grip of fear, trying to keep a grip on yourself, the urgent but futile project of gripping your children to keep them safe. For me as a writer, it even referred to my grip on this particular material, which always felt a little tenuous.

"Grip": short, apt, evocative, and easy to recall. I kept questioning and testing its rightness throughout the revision process, but it stuck.

POV

One writerly rule of thumb is not to switch POV in tight quarters, so I worried over the last section of "Grip." The piece opens by talking about "my son" in the third person but then pulls a swerve at the very end and speaks directly to him: "like these lines I will never show you, shielding you from the fear I carry—like a sort of oath I swore over your quiet sleep." The whole thing, I hope the reader can see at that point, has been addressed to him all along—but won't be disclosed to him. To know the pain and intensity your parents carry is too heavy a burden.

That's what I believed when I composed it, anyway. When I learned it was going to be on the air and might eventually be published, I worried. We'd had a bad moment a couple of years before, when a high school friend had told him something from *The Truth Book*. He had decided earlier not to read it, knowing from the subtitle (*Escaping a Childhood of Abuse among Jehovah's Witnesses*) that it would make him sad. I thought that was a healthy boundary for him to draw.

But then his friend read the book and asked him about something. When he came home, he cried. "Did that happen to you?" he said. It really hurt him.

I didn't want to put him through anything similar again, so I gave him a copy of "Grip" to read, and by then, he was older and in college and thought it was a good idea to do so. When he read it, he was pretty unfazed. Kids will surprise you.

The POV switch had troubled me from a technical standpoint, so

I tried a number of alternatives to make the piece more consistent, but nothing else felt true. I gave up temporarily, and when I read the piece aloud at Pine Manor with the POV shift intact, it didn't seem to baffle or bother anyone. I left it alone after that.

FORM

In form, I prefer short over long, the slap to the lecture.

This preference may come from being raised to be seen and not heard, raised as a girl in what was then a very male-dominated religion. Women were exhorted to be silent, and my family echoed that precept and enforced it with violence. In such a context, if you open your mouth, you'd better have something important to say.

Of course, I don't agree with that now, but it was my world from birth to fourteen, and it had its effect on my aesthetic. Although I've been a professor for twelve years, the lectern remains an uneasy space for me (even though I now say things like "space"). Holding forth: very difficult. The sound of my own voice in public for any stretch of time makes me nervous, and it's that way on the page, too.

Also, I get bored easily, and I resent writers who bore me, so I don't want to bore anyone else.

Short works for me. Compression. Urgency. Get in, get out.

It's funny to me that this essay is longer than "Grip" itself.

PATIENCE

I always encourage students to let things lie. Let them settle. When you're going through the thick of something—whether you're breaking up your marriage or climbing Mount Kilimanjaro—it's hard to do anything except journalism. Take notes, sure. But don't try to force art from it. It's too close. You can't see it yet.

The patterns—the ones that really illuminate, reveal, show something new—don't emerge that quickly. They can take years to surface from the welter of immediate detail.

I was twenty-one when I hung that bullet-holed target over my son's crib, and it didn't strike me as macabre or even as a possible strange form of oath until my very late thirties, when I suddenly *saw* it: saw that dark target hanging there over the crib in my mind's eye and thought, for the first time, *Hey, that's weird. What was I thinking?* I saw it in conjunction with the fear I'd carried and my mother's attack by her abusive husband long after she'd left him, moved to another state, and believed herself safe. I could see her failure to protect my brother and me juxtaposed starkly against that black gun in my hands. But at twenty-one, I couldn't have told you any of that.

My son, as I write this, will be twenty-one himself in October. A lot of time has passed since the events "Grip" narrates.

What I'm saying is that it takes time to see. You have to acquire a different perspective to see your old self anew, to see the patterns that have been lying there all along.

The discipline of deep writing asks you to be patient. Don't rush your work; don't force it. Keep writing and reading while you wait.

I've been helped by teaching and studying literature from an analytical, scholarly standpoint. When I'm teaching a story by Daniel Chacón or a poem by Julia Alvarez, I have to approach it in a cool, neutral way to see how its parts work to make meaning and how the writer is re-creating a world in language.

Doing that constantly, for a living, could kill the creative impulse outright. The danger is that the work itself will become professorial: too suffused by the living death of committee meetings and the unacknowledged privilege of having the leisure to pick over small things at great length. I worry about that, but in the meantime, teaching and analyzing literature has schooled me to a kind of alertness about language and effect.

My goal now is to keep training, keep gaining skills: to write sonnets and haiku and villanelles—write a novel!—so that I'll have multiple techniques at my fingertips. Then, when something does strike me as genuinely provocative or strange, I hope I'll be able to bring it to the page.

Hungry

I came to college hungry.

"The kids look like they're in a concentration camp," a mutual friend told our father, who lived in another part of the state and had failed to get custody. During the late years of my childhood, literal starvation had been both a punishment and a way of life, enforced by our abusive Jehovah's Witness stepfather and mother. Gaunt, malnourished, beaten, suffering from the lack of medical and dental care, my brother and I rattled around our classrooms, the school bus, the Kingdom Hall, and no one intervened. At fourteen, I ran away from that trailer, and with the police, the courts, and my father's help, we got my little brother out. For two more years, I lived with my father and his wife, devouring tuna, wheat bread, peanut butter, putting on weight, putting on the clothes they bought for me in bulk at the outlet store, since I'd run away with nothing.

With time, I began to pass for normal. I was the only Latina I knew at my West Virginia high school, but with my pale skin and dark hair and eyes, I looked like just another Italian American, a descendant of those waves of immigrants who'd come to work the mountains' coal mines. Some of my high-school friends went into the mines themselves. Some joined the military. By graduation, many of the girls were engaged.

I came to college hungry for knowledge, for experience.

Jehovah's Witnesses don't believe in evolution, don't participate in politics, don't celebrate any of the myriad Judeo-Christian traditional holidays that brighten most people's lives in the United States: birthdays, Christmas, Chanukah, Easter, Thanksgiving. Intellectually, I was nearly a blank slate, and eager to fill in the gaps, but Jehovah's Witnesses don't believe that college is necessary, and my mother had always forbidden me to dream of it. For me, she envisioned only a good, virginal marriage in the Kingdom Hall and a life of stay-at-home motherhood, of scripture and subservience, of knowing my place and keeping it. In return, I'd be rewarded—eventually—with eternal life on a perfect paradise earth, unburdened by racial injustice, poverty, environmental degradation, or war.

It was the same promise that had lured my Cuban American grandmother away from Catholicism when a Jehovah's Witness climbed the steps of her front porch long ago. A Key West housewife with a seventh-grade education, raising five children and caring for more, my *abuela* chose an idealized vision of this life, this earth—and for her children: peace, justice, and plenty. She died clinging to that dream.

I have not kept my place. Like my mother and grandmother, I chose the earth—but the real earth, complicated and torn, not a post-Armageddon fantasy purveyed by a global religious organization with its own political and financial ends. I chose education, although, growing up, I knew no one who had graduated from college, aside from my schoolteachers and, briefly, my father's lawyer. My parents had only their high school diplomas. None of my relatives and none of my parents' friends had been to college. It was a mysterious, forbidden world, which is perhaps why I wanted it so badly. I chose worldly knowledge and worldly pleasures—and, since my father believed you didn't need a college education, much less graduate school, I did it at my own expense, with generous scholarships, tedious jobs, and enormous loans.

This labor and debt often set me apart from my friends at the groomed green campus of the elite university in Texas that I attended, a school that liked to be called the Harvard of the South and was renowned for golf and tennis—rich people's sports, games I couldn't play. There were no Latina sororities at my university then, and the sororities that did exist seemed stocked with a breed of weird, beautiful aliens. I couldn't relate. I hung out mostly with other scholarship kids, but even they tended to come from comfortable middle-class homes.

When I became pregnant at twenty, the baby's father and I moved into a two-hundred-dollar-a-month apartment in a predominantly Mexican American barrio. My college friends stopped coming around. Most of them who entered my new neighborhood did so only to buy drugs.

But while the area had its problems with crime—the drugs, the wooden houses lit ablaze, the occasional gunshot—there were things about it that I liked. The landlord had my brother's name, and I liked the alleys where women in dusty backyards trimmed their husbands' hair. I liked our sweet neighbors Meiyo and Yoli, finding myself more at ease with them than with my college peers who drove Volvos and Mercedes and went to Vail for spring break. I liked lugging the baby on one hip and the laundry on the other down the rickety wooden stairs and across the street to the open-air laundromat—just a couple of washers and dryers in a guy's carport—and chatting in my battered Spanglish with the other mamas. The crime did scare me, true—but I felt sort of at home.

Yet I felt sort of at home, too, in the seminar rooms at the university, arguing about the politics of texts, or doing research in the library. My mind felt like it was finally stretching and working in the way it was born to work. Though my professors did not, in the 1980s, offer courses on Latina/o literature or women's literature or working-class literature, I could still use the skills I learned to analyze the literature of my own choosing. I rode the bus back and forth between the manicured campus and my shabby street, confused but happy.

Two homes. Sort of. As Latinas in higher education, we don't have to make an either-or choice about what we want or who we will become. We can choose to be both-and. Our challenge is finding and balancing the right ingredients: the ones that nourish us, the ones that taste right.

Today I am a professor with a joint appointment in English and ethnic studies. I teach Latina/o literature, Latina/o studies, women's literature, and creative writing, and I move with comfort and pleasure between my two departments. The student body at the university in Nebraska where I teach is over 90 percent non-Hispanic white, but I'm okay with that. I'm used to it, and I can be useful here, sharing texts, ideas, and perspectives with students who wouldn't otherwise encounter them—and nurturing and mentoring with special pride those Latino and Latina students who do make it through the door. I can help make college a place where they can envision themselves, a place where they, too, can feel at home. I can help recruit them and tell them the truth about the hard parts as well as the rewards.

I went to college at sixteen, hungry for so many things. Now in my forties, I have tasted so much. So much has nourished me. And I am still hungry, still learning.

On Becoming Educated

In graduate school in the 1990s, I am introduced to a feminist professor of law. We're in a bagel shop. It's sunny. Wiry, with cropped sandy hair and glasses, she looks exactly like my nascent concept of a feminist.

She's working on an article about a little-known provision in the Violence Against Women Act, which President Clinton has just signed into law. The new legislation makes employers responsible for providing workplace protection for women whose partners have threatened them with violence. In the past, violent men had ignored restraining orders to assault and even kill women at their workplaces. This new legislation requires employers, if notified that a targeted woman is in their employ, to provide appropriate security rather than leaving it to the individual woman to defend herself.

I know about men who hurt women.

This is marvelous, I tell the professor. Her article will help protect thousands of women—hundreds of thousands, maybe. I think of my mother, my friend Cindy, my neighbor Diana. Battering happens in every stratum of society, but under the poverty level, domestic violence increases by a factor of five. In the trailer park and barrio and rural towns where I've lived, I've seen my share.

But the professor grimaces and shakes her head. Her article, she explains, is for a law journal, an academic journal. Only other scholars will read it.

But since this new legislative provision isn't widely known, I suggest she could write an article for a mass-market women's magazine, one that will reach millions of women. Not *Ms.*, which is hard to find, but the kind of magazine available at drugstores and supermarkets, the kind that sits in stacks at inexpensive beauty salons, *Cosmopolitan* or *Redbook*; the kind that reaches ordinary women, women who might be getting beaten. She could save actual women's lives.

Her face wrinkles. That's not the kind of article she writes, she explains with exaggerated patience. Someone else will do that, eventually. A writer who does commercial, popular articles for a general audience.

Her own work, she says, will trickle down.

I take a graduate course in feminist theory. Our professor, educated at one of the world's most prestigious universities, is intimidatingly brilliant in the seminar she runs like a Socratic inquisition one evening a week. I admire her; I like her; I want to be her—but as the semester winds on, my eagerness dissipates because I don't understand Toril Moi or Luce Irigaray or any of the feminists (after Virginia Woolf) whose work we're reading.

I'm a first-generation college student, here by fluke on fellowship, and the theorists' English seems foreign to me, filled with jargon and abstractions at which I can only guess. They say nothing about wife-beating or rape or unequal wages or child molesting, which is the charge that finally got my stepfather sent to prison. They say nothing about being a single mother on ten thousand dollars a year, which is my own situation. The feminist writers respond to male theorists—Lacan, Derrida—whose work I haven't read. I can't parse their sentences or recognize their allusions, and I don't know what they mean or how they're helpful to the strippers and dropouts and waitresses I know, the women I care about the most, to my aunt Lettie who worked the register at Winn-Dixie and my aunt Linda who cleaned houses.

It's true that the complexity and jargon are alluring, like another country, safe and leisured, with a strange, beautiful language that means only abstract things, where a dozen bright young women and their interlocutor can spend three hours conversing around a big table in a comfortable, air-conditioned room that looks like a corporate boardroom in a movie. But I climb the stairs each week in grim frustration.

bell hooks's piece "Out of the Academy and Into the Streets" appears in *Ms.*, and I'm relieved that someone has expressed the inchoate things rumbling inside me. I make photocopies and take it to my professor, asking if we could please read and discuss it in class. She takes the copies and says she'll see.

One evening, our discussion has strayed to Stephen Greenblatt, who, I'll learn later, is the paradigm-shifting Renaissance scholar who initiated New Historicism, a scholarly approach to literary texts. At the time, I know none of this; he's just another male name. I have no context, but the professor and some of the older students seem to have read his work, perhaps in other classes. The professor is intense, lively. She presses her fist to the seminar table. "How do we, as feminist theorists, *respond* to Stephen Greenblatt?"

"What if we don't respond?" I say in frustration. "What if we just keep working on issues that are focused on actual women, issues we actually care about?"

Her eyes are wide. "You can't just *ignore* Stephen Greenblatt," she says. The oldest graduate student, the smart one I admire, shakes her head and smiles faintly.

I disengage. At the end of the term, I write my paper on Woolf's *A Room of One's Own*, the only book that was clear to me.

We never do discuss the piece by bell hooks.

In a different class, a graduate seminar on multicultural literature, our professor assigns Gloria Anzaldúa's *Borderlands/La Frontera: The New Mestiza*. I enter the seminar room that day with excitement. For the first time in my graduate career, I've encountered a text that speaks passionately to me, a text radical and thrilling, an author whose feminist, ethnic, sexual, and working-class concerns correspond to my own, a book that acknowledges real-world prejudice, poverty, and sexual violation, that mixes poetry and history, memoir and argument. I have fallen in love. In cursive, I've gushed onto the title page of the black paperback: *The most incredible book I've ever read. It speaks straight to me.*

At last. I can't wait to talk about it.

But the professor, whom I've always admired, opens class by apologizing for having assigned the book at all. He'd included it, he explains, only because he'd heard it was important. But if he'd read it first, he would never have put it on the syllabus: it was too disjointed, too polemical. Students quickly chime in with their discomfort over the book's "angry" content.

I'm confused. My professor and classmates hadn't stumbled over W. E. B. DuBois, Zora Neale Hurston, or Maxine Hong Kingston, but Gloria Anzaldúa is somehow too different, too much.

It's the anger in the text, I learn, that bothers them. "She's so *angry*," they keep saying. For the whole session, I find myself arguing in defense of the book's worth, trying to articulate the difference between being angry by temperament and expressing justified anger in response to violation.

The experience is both alienating and illuminating. *Did you think we weren't angry?*

Maybe if you're a distinguished professor of law, the notion of your name next to a piece in *Cosmo* makes you cringe. Maybe if your educational pedigree is immaculate, the remedial intellectual needs of people who grew up with food stamps aren't your problem. Maybe if you're a well-meaning professor teaching ethnic literature, Anzaldúa's anger is the only thing visible. Maybe you can't feel the burn of every injustice she inherited and lived, much less appreciate the elegance of her complex aesthetic.

At the time, I didn't realize that these small incidents were negotiations of power, contests over whose perspectives mattered and whose voices would be permitted and welcomed at the table. At the institution where I did my graduate work in the 1990s, Third World feminism, women-of-color feminism, and transnational feminism hadn't yet trickled down.

After earning a doctorate, I was hired by a small men's college in rural Indiana. At Wabash, which prided itself on its maintenance of tradition, men comprised not only the entire student body but also most of the faculty and almost the whole administrative structure.

Students asked, while I was sitting at my desk in my office, whose secretary I was. Alumni at luncheons asked what a "purty young thing" like me was doing there. All-campus emails by drunk freshmen asked for the best place on campus to beat their meat.

I taught there for ten years, the only tenure-line woman in my department for the first nine. I earned tenure; I chaired my department. We hired more women.

I also got to teach women's literature, including Latina literature, and feminist theory to classrooms of thirty-five men at a time. Farmboys and lawyers' sons took my classes. Some came with the expressed intention of debunking feminism. Some wanted to know, when we read the novels of Jean Rhys, why we had to read a book by a slut. Some questioned women's right to vote. Yes. When I taught Gloria Anzaldúa's *Borderlands/La Frontera*, I was under no illusion that its insights would be met with joy.

I value those voices, those questions, that red-state hostility, because they taught me how to make feminism's insights relevant to people outside a closed, snug room of agreement. I learned how to make feminist theory, critical race theory, and observations about class privilege relevant, exciting, and even needful to people who had no material reason to care. I learned diplomacy. I learned not to back down.

As academics, we can forget the urgency and hunger people have for the knowledge we hold. We can forget that even those who claim to be hostile may need what we offer to help them make sense of a complicated world.

Academics don't share a monolithic experience. Many of us are adjuncts or lecturers, forced to piece together work with few benefits and little security, while the fortunate percentage of us with tenure-track positions have to hustle to build our vitas and merit files as our institutions require. Either way, the thick busyness of our lives can induce a sweet, privileged forgetfulness, a smug sense of how worthwhile our work of "knowledge production" is. Over the years, I've known many dedicated and creative teachers, eager to reach and engage every student, yet I've also known academics who view students as an obstacle to their real work of research or see teaching as a process of simply culling the best from the herd.

But I speak now as one of that herd. The herd is made up of smart, desperate, and intellectually eager individuals—if they are met halfway, if they are spoken to with respect and in language they can understand. They have not been to Harvard, and if we make them feel stupid, inadequate, and ashamed for not knowing its vocabularies and sharing its assumptions, they will retreat. (My brother, living in a trailer with friends and putting himself through college, dropped out after a year.) If our concerns seem too abstract, effete, and irrelevant, they will turn away in disgust.

Yet we need them. Their voices are vital. The academy—as we fondly, misguidedly call it, as if it were some great, unified thing—is lumbering along amid eviscerating budget cuts, pressures to corporatize, to streamline, to justify its existence to hostile anti-intellectual factions and a skeptical public, to become purely instrumental, a machine that grants job credentials to twenty-two-year-olds so they can get on with their lives. In the face of such intense and varied pressures, the academy must find ways to preserve itself as a place for thought to flourish—yet *everyone* needs to be invited to think. The discussion has to matter to everyone, and everyone's voice must be heard.

Last spring, my son graduated from Oberlin College, and in only a few more months, I'll have paid off my own enormous student loans. That is, I believe deeply in the intellectual benefits of higher education and have willingly indentured myself to attain them. On the other hand, I loathe the academy's blind spots.

A few years ago, Stephen Greenblatt—*the* Stephen Greenblatt— said in an interview, "I've been at this for 40 years. And, as an academic, I've been content with relatively small audiences, with the thought that the audience I long for will find its way eventually to what I have written, provided that what I have written is good enough."

On the one hand, there's a lovely quiet confidence in the long view Greenblatt takes, a modest surety of purpose, but it's also a position freighted with an absence of urgency. That unacknowledged absence is a luxury, a privilege, that too many academics ignore, not at their own peril, but at the peril of others, others like the women who would have been very grateful to learn about that provision in the Violence Against Women Act about employers' responsibilities to protect them. "The audience I long for will find its way eventually to what I have written," Greenblatt writes. *Eventually.* There's no rush. And the burden of finding knowledge, you'll note, is on the audience. Seeking the audience out is not configured as the thinker's job. *Eventually, if I am superb enough, the chosen few will manage to discover my work.*

Sitting on my sofa on a Saturday morning, writing, it still surprises and honors me that an editor has asked me to write an essay for a prestigious college's online journal. I was raised to be seen and not heard. Now someone wants my voice?

That's the key, I think: to remain surprised, to remain honored. Our public voices are an extraordinary privilege. We can make the choice to carry with us and be shaped by the voices we've heard—the strippers and dropouts and battered mothers—and we can act so that what we do will matter to them. We can continue to choose—no matter what islands of remove our positions may afford us—to keep inviting those voices: to teach free classes to the poor, for example, and to listen to what the poor tell us when they read our cherished texts. We can teach texts written by poor women in our classrooms. We can remember that torture and abuse traumatize humans into silence, and that humiliation and subordination train people into reticence, but that their voices, those valuable voices, can be fished to the surface again, if we are patient, if we are kind. If we care.

In graduate school, professors said you had to choose one thing or the other: you could be a creative writer or a scholar, not both. The creative writing professors said you had to choose a genre: poetry or fiction, not both. You could be a feminist professor in a classroom or a feminist activist on the streets, not both.

It was all too reminiscent of the old divisions long demanded of us: you must think or feel, not both. You must be a mind or a body, not both. You can be pretty or smart, not both. You can have a family or a career. Why did intellectuals in the 1990s continue to invest in such reductive binaries? Why the urge to bifurcate, to build retaining walls between the multiple truths of our experience?

They were wrong. It isn't necessary. Today we publish scholarship and creative work. We write for general audiences and trained specialists in our field. We publish in glossy magazines, and the local newspaper, and academic journals; we publish scholarly articles, and poetry, and fiction, and memoir.

For me, all of feminism's waves and permutations—as well as the voices that contest it—are essential. All of our varied feminisms seek a more just world, and there's no need to limit our efforts to particular spheres, no need to cut ties with parts of ourselves. While I serve on the advisory board of a university press with other professors, vetting scholarly projects for publication, I also serve as a mentor to a Latina-Lakota teenager whose mother, a meth addict, lost custody.

She lives with her father, stepmother, and two brothers in their small mobile home in a trailer park. When I drive to see her, it feels like I am driving into my own past.

Vesper Adest

Skin at the ankles is soft. Smooth under the lips, vulnerable. Softer, thinner than his skin was in his twenties.

Nearly two decades now, kissing the same ankles, feeling their skin thinning under my lips, slow as erosion, as sandstone scrubbed by water into silk.

When I was twenty-one, a middle-aged woman tried to counsel me. She loved to clog, and, oh, to clog with friends on a sunny day—well, life didn't get much better than that! I should seek such controllable joys, she said: my life would calm down. I thought she was barking mad. Her mouse-brown hair was thin, and she wore socks under her sandals. What could she possibly teach me? I sought the wild arch of ecstasy, the mind's last fuse blown.

I'm forty-one now. My hips and knees ache after I run. When I can bring myself to run.

Krishna, understanding women, hologrammed himself onto the banks of the holy Ganges: one hundred Krishnas, one for each gopi, fresh, eager, soft-muzzled as the cows they tended, sinking to grass under India's moon to beat out the phrases of glory. Even Jesus left behind a harem, those wimpled nuns. They slid willing fingers into literal rings and swore to cleave to Him as wives unto their husbands.

Fidelity is an art of the body—not, as some would have it, a discipline of the will. My upbringing made me prone to stray. To stay, I had to remake myself in a new image, one that dwelt, not a traveler. How to explore the same country, again and again?

But it's never the same river twice. Taste it.

Hot Monogamy, one book is called. *Tepid Monogamy*: no one has written that. *Merely Comfy Monogamy*. Imagine the sales figures. See the heads of editors roll.

In youth, we both were blessed with rude health, if not much else. Rude health and looks another century would have called blooming. We bloomed, then.

Now the surgeries, fear, the smell of fear, of illness, of infection. *Sickness and in health*. The medicines on the counter, the cleaning up. The care of the body, its tender messes, the helplessness of what was virile and brave now breaking, now mending, now broken, just broken. The soft grief of watching.

The beauty of a fading thing—it takes a delicate eye, and my taste never ran to sepia or petals pressed in books. How strange to watch the glossy territory of his hair be gained, thread by thread, by silver. To watch the pink gums' nearly imperceptible recession. Is that disgusting, to say that? Is it un-American to find him lovely still, though his arms are less muscled, his thews less thick, the scleras of his eyes less clear, more vesseled red? Even his scent is milder now. I stand and breathe the dark places of his throat, feeling alive and tenuous on the earth. The arches of my feet lift and shiver.

A Sunday slicked with gray rain, a quiet arm around me, a held hand. The kindness of his gaze when I am naked, the knowingness of our embrace. It all sounds dull, put down here. How can I show you? It is not dull. *Happily ever after* conceals a world. Conceals the chair I smashed against his wall, gashing the wood, shattering the legs. It couldn't be repaired. Married people keep on having a story, you know. It's not all tea and toast.

The skin of his inner forearm. Of his wrist. The soft salt hollow at the back of his knee. The simple wonder of skin, that barrier, that necessary web stretched between what pulses within—all the dark, mute viscera, churning—and the great sharp airy world outside. Our skin, the river of sensation where we meet—where I can touch you, and you feel it. Extraordinary, this gift.

His skin in youth, like thick satin. Rugged, smooth. Now: softer, lighter. As if thinning toward translucence. As if beaten gold.

We are not old yet. With luck, we will be. With luck, we will find old age together, our eyes open, our forgiving gaze opening in welcome, seeing the thinning softening fading flesh so beautiful, still so beautiful, as we thresh our gentle way toward rest.

Famous men have always written of the beauty of women, how poignant or pitiable or repulsive its twilight is, how the loathsomeness of pleating flesh drives them to withdraw their shrinking love and find someone fresh, a girl smooth and buoyant with promise.

For me to gaze back, then—to see the man's aging body, to fail to loathe it, and not to fret about my own: is that a radical act? A strike against fascism? I don't feel bad about my neck.

You didn't need to grow old to know that skin and soul are inextricable. You didn't need to burn your books to learn: the spirit loves the flesh, the pulse, the muscle clutch, the tremor in the skin.

Not glamour. Not the body in extremis, in childbirth, in torture, in fever, or buckling under the belt. Not heroic, swimming cold seas, cycling New Zealand, tearing the finish-line tape. Not the body rent. Hurt, opened, with its metal purple heart. Not the body as live porn, pumping or pole-dancing, strutting, stripping.

But the body cherished, ordinary, going about its daily song, loved, kind, growing older. The body at peace, cared for. Tended as one tends a garden. *Flesh of my flesh*. Those ankles, kissed. Shimmering with light.

As children, we were right: Here is the church, here the steeple.

The temple? These bones, robed with now.

"¿Quién es ese Jimmy Choo?"

A Latina Mother Comes of Age

Three years ago, at the age of thirty-nine, I looked up.

My only son had left for college, and I had earned tenure and was chairing my department at a small college. My nest was suddenly empty, and my days, though busy and full, were less frantic than they'd been while I was climbing the academic ladder. Suddenly I could exhale, and I raised my head and looked around.

In my family of origin, as the oldest child and a girl, I had been pressed into mothering service early. When my Cuban American father left us for a younger woman, our deeply religious mother struggled with low-paying jobs, a series of troubled relationships, and shame. Carrying too many burdens of her own, she was unable to mother us well. While she worked long hours, I spent my childhood raising my little brother Tony and striving for good grades. Though I adored my brother, he was reckless and curious; it took all my attention to keep him safe. My path was a clear one: as long as I kept my brother and myself clean, fed, and out of trouble, our mother was pleased.

One of the punishments she'd imposed when I was quite small—even before my brother was born—was to take and throw away one of my stuffed toys each time I said, "I can't." If I was unable to accomplish alone some chore she'd told me to do or something a teacher had assigned, I had no options: I had to keep working until I'd achieved it on my own. Giving up, admitting failure, and receiving help were all equally out of the question.

This promoted a certain self-sufficiency, which came in handy.

My whole identity thus crystallized early around the ideas of achievement at school and selflessness at home, of sacrifice as a virtue, of putting first the care of others. Placing someone else's needs at the center of my existence became safe, comfortable, familiar. It felt right; it felt like home. There was a space carved in me for motherhood long before I could have children.

Forbidden to go to college, I ran away and eventually went anyway, guilty about leaving my brother behind but hopeful for a new life and excited about the prestigious institution that had accepted me. But as a first-generation college student—a scholarship girl working two jobs—I felt overwhelmed by the Volvos and ski trips my new friends took for granted. It all looked marvelous, but I couldn't see my way forward into such a life. I felt a restless anxiety. Who was I? How could I prioritize? What did I want?

It was only a matter of time, I suppose, before I re-created the emotionally familiar pattern of my childhood. At twenty, I became pregnant—the only pregnant student visible on our country-club campus.

One of our culture's ugly open secrets is that girls who are sexually abused, as I was by my stepfather, have a higher incidence of un-planned pregnancy, their personal boundaries shattered by violation, their sense of worth linked to premature sexualization. But only years later did I learn that. At twenty, my achievements in college struggled against that same undertow in me. I often wonder how much of the blame and moral outrage our society directs at girls for their teen pregnancies—especially poor girls, especially girls of color—should be laid at the door of the selfish older men who got there first—and who leave the girls feeling so guilty, dirtied, and silenced that they accept society's censure and disgust.

I did finish college, and I raised my son while pursuing a master's degree and then a doctorate in literature. While graduate school challenged my intellect, so did mothering, which was, for me, both scholarly and creative. Scholarly, in that I carefully researched how to do things differently from the way my parents did: I took a university course in child psychology and read hungrily on my own about attachment parenting, self-esteem, and how to raise children without wielding corporal punishment, deprivation, or verbal abuse.

Mothering was also creative in that, because of my love for my son—my simple interest in his life and little experiences and fresh, poetic ways of seeing the world—I invented new strategies to keep Grey happy and safe, yet still acceptable to social norms. Profanities, for example, became "bathtub words," which he was free to yell with impunity as long as he was standing in our empty bathtub. His "restaurant voice" had a volume dial, which we turned low for public settings. In stores, a "two-finger stroke"—no thumbs—allowed him to touch tempting objects without picking them up and thus imperiling them. I loved inventing little strategies that let him meet his needs while not impinging upon other people. And the love that streamed back from him soothed my hurt heart. Hugging, playing at the park, singing him to sleep each night—motherhood provided a thousand ways to practice kindness, patience, empathy, and imagination. Doing these things as a single mother living below the poverty line (at ten thousand and then twelve thousand dollars a year in the 1990s) was difficult, yet I value that experience not only for its personal rewards but also because it connects me with struggling mothers all over the world whose love and invention exist on a shoestring. For me, there has been no more joyous, challenging work than raising my child.

At twenty-eight, I married the man of my dreams, who was also from a modest background. Feeling responsible for my son's support and faced with a tough academic market, I took the first tenure-track job offered, even when it turned out to come from a men's college in a small Indiana town. As someone born in Miami and educated in Texas, where I spent thirteen years, I had begun to take sunshine and the presence of Latinos and Latinas for granted. *Rural Indiana*, I thought. *How bad can it be?*

But the cold, gray Midwest nearly flattened me. For ten years, I taught theory, literature, and creative writing to young men. My colleagues were nearly all men and almost all Anglo. Female colleagues my own age tended to leave the institution after a year or two, so I was lonely for friendship. During my decade there, I knew only one other Latina on the faculty, and she wasn't granted tenure. Students complained about her accent. But I stayed on, determined to earn the college tuition remission benefit for my son, eager to spare him the debt, poverty, and grind of my own collegiate experience. I focused on appreciating the good colleagues and mentors I had, and on learning to teach well in a challenging environment.

Dignidad made my husband and me reluctant to seek financial credit, aside from a mortgage, so for those ten years in Indiana, we paid down our student loans, shared one Honda, watched one boxy old TV, and managed to afford (to my permanent regret) only one family vacation. But we paid cash for our lives, and we were proud of that. Nurturing, studying, and making ends meet on a strict, bleak budget were all I knew, all I had ever known.

When our son left for college, I took a breath and looked around, wondering what to do with the time and emotional energy that his leaving would grant me. What does a thirty-nine-year-old woman do with herself?

Apparently, according to the films and TV shows I suddenly had time to watch, thirty-nine-year-old women got manicures, went shoe shopping, flirted, dated, deluded themselves about romance, kvetched endlessly to friends, of which they seemed to have a steady supply, and wore confectionary little frocks to a whirl of parties, cocktails, and pricey restaurants. Even the Latina versions of this pop-culture narrative of femininity, like *Latina* magazine or Alisa Valdes-Rodriguez's *The Dirty Girls Social Club* and a host of chica-lit imitators, offered only more of the same. With new leisure to peer at popular culture, I felt dazzled and bewildered.

It all looked delectable—and made me feel dull and drab. Raised to put *familia* first, my energies had centered tightly on my son, my career, and my marriage—in precisely that order, as my good-humored husband would attest. My committed feminism was real but virtual: it came from books and my university professors, not from relationships with actual women. I had few female friends, much less Latina friends, and I didn't own any party dresses—too expensive, *verdad*—and anyway, who threw parties worth dressing up for in our small rural town? A son to raise plus a sixty-hour work week left no time for leisurely brunches full of *chisme* or girls'-day-out pedicures, much less weekend getaways with friends to get "pampered," which seemed to be a watchword of feminine culture but reminded me only of diapers.

I love my son, my work, my husband—who is funny, smart, and kind, and who cooks. We have our health. *Tengo fe*. I am blessed in many ways.

But what I'm trying to identify, articulate, and record here is a transitional moment, a specific moment of dissonance and confusion that occurred when I looked out from my nest of *familia* and *libros* and saw a culture I didn't recognize, a culture that didn't recognize me. In a pop-culture kaleidoscope of feminized glamour and consumption, where was my place? What should I do with my newfound time and energy? Looking ahead to a future when my son would be finished with college, how would I spend or invest the sudden influx of disposable income, entirely new to me? On designer shoes? On-screen actresses and chica-lit heroines everywhere dropped brand names with ease and rapture: Christian Louboutin with their iconic red soles, Manolo Blahnik, Jimmy Choo. The bones of my own feet, widened long ago by pregnancy, didn't relish the thought.

Isolated from other Latinas—from other women, generally—I cannot claim my experience as representative or typical, and it was foolish, perhaps, to look to popular culture for images that would stimulate and refresh my imagination as I tried to envision new pos-sible selves, but I had few real women around me. Long experience as a feminist in the academy had trained me to read pop culture's images critically, but I was still disappointed by the options that appeared to be on offer.

I sat in the strange quiet of our empty house, feeling the swell of a very old anxiety, one I hadn't felt since before my son was born. Without motherhood to consume my time, energy, and thoughts, who was I? Without *la Virgen* to emulate, where was my path? Con-sumed by nearly unbearable anxiety, I felt an urgent need to find something, to latch onto some new and all-consuming good cause—another baby! the environmental movement! the Obama campaign! my brother Tony's new little son!—anything I could install as the new center of my life, anything into which I could throw myself to assuage the ache that gnawed my belly. Unmoored, I felt an uneasy inertia, as I had in my first years of college. How could I choose a future based merely on only my own wishes, desires? What *were* my desires? I felt rudderless, un-compassed, afraid of the vast range of choices that faced me.

Gloria Anzaldúa has described such strange, transitional states with the Nahuatl term *Nepantla*: a space of in-between-ness, or, as Graciela Slepoy puts it, "the interstice or passageway in the geography of the self that contains the potential for self-transformation." I was between roles, between goals, between the self I had been and a new self I could not yet envision. Anzaldúa uses a birth metaphor to describe the experience, seeing Nepantla as a "birthing stage where you feel like you're reconfiguring your identity and don't know where you are. You used to be this person but now you're different in some way. You're changing worlds and cultures and maybe classes, sexual preferences. So you go through this birthing of Nepantla. When you're in the midst of the Coatlicue state—the cave, the dark—you're hibernating or hiding, you're gestating and giving birth to yourself."

Three years ago, I was in the thick of my own Coatlicue state, yet it was a difficult thing to communicate to anyone. Our public roles require us to perform clarity, confidence, and certainty, while such transitional periods in our lives are colored instead by confusion, reevaluation, searching, and doubt. *In the middle of the road of my life*, as Dante famously wrote, *I awoke in a dark wood*. But being lost is a difficult thing to admit, especially when one is a full-fledged adult in professional midstride—and a parent, no less: someone who's supposed to know the way.

What I decided to do was sit with it. Sit and watch and think. I observed my own feelings and wondered about them, tracing their sources to the way I was raised and the things I was taught to believe. I looked at the way I had served and adored the male figures in my family—my father, my brother, my son—and how my attention and priorities had revolved around them since almost the dawn of my memory. I considered the strange irony of my teaching Latina literature and feminist theory at an all-male, mostly Anglo college. However beloved my brother and son, however meaningful my work with male students, I wondered if I wanted my future energies to continue to tend the masculine.

While examining my interior structures of belief, I also continued to look outward at the images of women our culture purveys. The white, middle-class empty nesters whose stories the media covers and who look forward to travel and golf were a decade or more older than I, while the never-childed women who flitted glamorously onscreen seemed much younger, even when they were the same chronological age. Though the occasional woman of color was thrown in for dash, like a spice, most characters were Anglo, and for all their sorority-sister-style bonding, they pursued the individualistic American Dream, every woman for herself. Even most chica lit purveyed only a thinly Latinized vision of the same.

My experiences make me prioritize *familia*, community, social justice, *dignidad*, and spirituality over conspicuous consumption and luxury, sweet though those might sometimes appear after a hard week. Frivolity must be cultivated, I think, if it is to flourish: one must suspend or bracket one's judgment and values, as well as one's knowledge of the fact that people elsewhere are hungry. The behavior and values displayed by the mass-media caricatures of women—including Latina women, such as the character Gabrielle Solis on *Desperate Housewives*—seemed to be those of extended adolescence, and while some of it looked like fun, much just appeared childish. My life experience had given me little practice at frivolity. What I found was that, even when faced with the opportunity, I had no real desire to indulge.

I knew I wanted community, the feminine, the warmth of *latinidad*. But I didn't know how to get there.

In 2006, I made a choice that changed my life. Nominated for admission to the Macondo Writing Workshop in San Antonio, I went. I remember standing up, nervous and trembling, to introduce myself to the sixty or so other writers. We had been asked to say a few words about how and why we write. I said that I write into what scares me—as I am doing now—and sat down quickly.

Limited to writers committed to social justice, Macondo (named in tribute to Gabriel García Márquez's village Macondo in *One Hundred Years of Solitude*) is the brainchild of author Sandra Cisneros, with whom I studied there. Sandra's generosity extended past the classroom; she invited us to her home in the King William district, which was full of bright, lush colors and art. As I walked quietly through, admiring everything, my Indiana home suddenly began to seem drab and pale. Safe, bland, quiet. Beige. I remembered how my son had wanted for his bedroom the room I'd eyed for a study, and how quickly I'd relinquished it, wanting him to feel happy in our new place.

I wondered how to stop relinquishing.

In our workshop, Sandra warned us not to be consumed by our community activism or political work. "If you are a writer," she told us, "then writing is the most important political work you can do." I wrote it in my notebook and stared at it for long minutes, repeating it over and over again in my inner ear. It didn't seem quite right, quite okay. Writing? Creative writing, which I loved and had been doing on the side as a kind of delightful vice while I'd been teaching literature and publishing criticism? My little stories—politically significant? Could this be the direction in which I should turn my energies? I'd been publishing fiction and essays since graduate school, and my first book had recently come out, but writing was not an acknowledged priority in my heart or in my daily schedule.

I thought of Virginia Woolf's *A Room of One's Own*, the feminist classic that insists a woman must have a room of her own in which to write, and of Sandra's chapter "A House of My Own" in *The House on Mango Street*, which takes the principle a significant step further—a whole house, not just a room—and claims that desire in the first person: "Not a man's house. Not a daddy's. A house all my own. With my porch and my pillow, my pretty purple petunias." I thought of the way I had no study in our house, of the way I carried my notebook from porch to living room to kitchen table, wherever there was a quiet spot.

I flew home to my empty nest in Indiana with an open mind. That's all I was: open. That's all I had the energy to be, I realized with surprise. I was exhausted—something I hadn't admitted to anyone, my mother's prohibitions against "I can't" still looming large in my psyche. Exhausted, but open. So I watched and waited, quiescent, alert.

And then that fall, sitting on the sofa on a gray Saturday morning, I received a phone call from someone I barely knew. Her name was Amelia María de la Luz Montes, and she'd been at Macondo, too. She'd read my work and heard my self-introduction. She explained that she was the English Department's recruitment chair at the University of Nebraska–Lincoln and that they were looking for someone to fill a joint appointment in literature and Latino studies.

Would I ever be willing to consider, she asked, moving to Nebraska?

Today my husband and I live in a small apartment in downtown Lincoln. Bright paintings hang on our walls of soft gold. From our living room window, I can see the university.

Through a series of conscious choices and serendipitous unfoldings, my life is beginning to reconfigure itself around a model not of Latina mothering but of Latina sistering. I deliberately use the verb *sistering* rather than the noun *sisterhood* because for me it's an active, emerging process that I'm discovering as I go, rather than a received, readymade role into which one steps. I also mean *sistering* not in the second-wave, sisterhood-is-powerful way, though I am deeply influenced by and grateful for that model, and not in the pop-cultural *Sex and the City* mode of romanticized feminine friendships, but in a smaller, quirkier, more personal fashion, a multipronged approach that honors work, political commitment, community, and creativity.

Because I lost the benefit of tuition remission for my son when I left my former job, my budget is even tighter, so our apartment is tiny: I still don't have a room of my own. But the living room has an alcove where I work, and on the wall at my shoulder are images of virgin mothers—la Virgen de Guadalupe, but also la Virgen de la Caridad del Cobre from Cuba, and Spain's black Virgin of Montserrat. But they are mixed in with images by and of artists who never became mothers, like Remedios Varo and Frida Kahlo, whose large black-and-white photographic portrait broods over my screen as I type. A rosary and a strand of agave fiber (with its spiked brown tip still attached—nature's needle-and-thread) hang within easy reach. When I get stalled, I rub their comforting textures between my fingers and thumb. It's a space, at least, of my own.

Once, I dreamed up strategies on my son's behalf. Now I'm tentatively inventing structures for myself.

In the mornings, I walk to work, where I teach Latina and Latino studies and literature. Amelia, a creative writer who directs the ethnic studies program (we both have joint appointments), publishes scholarship on nineteenth-century California novelist María Amparo Ruiz de Burton and on Latina writers in the Great Plains and Midwest. When our English Department decided—*un milagro*—that it needed a critical mass of Latinas on the faculty, we brought in a new junior colleague, Ariana Vigil, who works on literature from the Central American civil wars of the 1980s. We go to dinner, share work, and widen our eyes at each other when faculty meetings get tedious or bizarre. This spring, we'll present a panel together in San Antonio about teaching Gloria Anzaldúa's *Borderlands/La Frontera: The New Mestiza*.

Once a month, I have dinner with anthropologist and ethnic studies colleague Carleen Sanchez, who excavates Mayan sites in Honduras and is working on a new study of Frida Kahlo. Like me, Carleen has a grown-up child, and like me, she's still young enough to wonder what's next—still young enough, with her red pumps, long black hair, and thick silver nose ring, to turn heads when she enters the restaurant. We start with wine at five o'clock and hug goodbye at midnight—but, unlike fictional women on TV shows, we don't talk about men or shopping (much). We talk about our work, teaching, politics, and culture. We do swap the occasional story about our children, but they're not our focal points. *We* are. What projects are we working on? How is teaching going? What recent headlines have aggrieved us? Carleen is a little older than I am, while I am a little farther along the tenure and promotion track than she is: our mentoring relationship, if it can be called that, is entirely mutual. Like a seesaw in the wind, its balance shifts and fluctuates as we take turns sharing knowledge and asking advice. Our conversations are long and serious—and fun.

Every Thursday evening, I pick up my fourteen-year-old Chicana-Honduran-Lakota Little Sister, with whom I was matched by the national Big Brothers, Big Sisters mentoring program. The oldest of five children of a single mother living in poverty, she has her own motherhood pitfalls to avoid: seven of her friends had babies last year, and her mother often left her alone to care for her young siblings, so caregiving is a familiar, comfortable practice for her, as it was for me. She faces other challenges, too; she has friends and family members in the Sureños street gang and in prison. We spend our evenings together talking about school, family, the "green-eyed Mexican sexies" she admires at her high school, and her dreams of being a pediatrician or marriage counselor. We play basketball at the Y, cook together, paint watercolors, go to coffee shops, restaurants, bookstores. We make each other laugh, and I can offer a safe shoulder when things get rough at home.

But no matter how fond I am of her or how much I'd like to transfuse some stability into her life of transience, violence, and multiple father-figures who come and go, I cannot whisk her away and install her at the center of my life. I cannot mother her. The terms of Big Brothers, Big Sisters dictate otherwise, and I'm grateful for those boundaries, grateful to learn how to care without being swallowed up. I cannot swoop in and save her; I'm required to drop her off at the end of the night. But I can be present for her, a Big Sister, a friend, an ally, another way for her to imagine her own future.

My cousin Jeri and I, born five days apart, once made mud pies and played like sisters in childhood, but we lost touch during my long years of childrearing and academic-ladder-climbing and Jeri's long years of serving as a Marine, working as a secretary, and then pursuing a college education in women's and environmental studies. We reconnected last year when I gave a reading in Miami, where Jeri now works for an international floral distributor, monitoring flower-growing centers in Colombia and other Latin American countries. We hope to travel together one day.

In the classroom, I mentor my students—particularly my Latina and Latino students—with affection and warmth, but I refrain from adopting a parental stance toward them. I've seen that approach misfire unhealthily in the lives of colleagues who view their students as emotional substitutes for children. Instead, I think of myself as someone just a little farther along the path my students want to follow, someone who can offer help, resources, advice, and cautionary tales, but who can't carry them.

Once a month, I meet my writing group for a long lunch: four women professors, two of whom—Amelia and I—are Latina. We share and critique manuscripts, but we also talk about our work in general and our personal lives. For me, our meetings are a lifeline, a time to take work and self seriously in a community of women, a chance to nurture, listen, and share in a way that doesn't privilege any of us at the expense of the others. We take turns caring and being nurtured, listening and being heard. Each of us shows her vulnerability; each of us shares her strength. Rather than mimicking the one-way nurturing of motherhood, we form a community of mutual kindness and respect.

The writing group has just finished critiquing, in fact, my lecture for an upcoming conference on the Americas. The conference's theme is immigration, and my lecture analyzes the differences between Josefina López's original stage version of *Real Women Have Curves* and the later version that made it to the screen, courtesy of HBO Films.

In the original stage play, five women in an ensemble cast learn from each other across divisions of age, experience, residency status, and cultural ambition. Ultimately, they empathize with and empower one another.

By contrast, the movie, which was substantially reshaped for a commercial mainstream audience, pits young Ana against her mother, Carmen, in a dyadic, agonistic struggle for control, which Ana finally wins. It's a satisfying triumph for viewers, but López's original views about immigration, female sexuality, and women's emotional and economic solidarity, as expressed in the stage play, are far more radical, exciting, and empowering than the muted, feel-good version that made it to the big screen and won awards.

The solidarity and empowerment of López's original vision are something I need to remember. Underneath the pop-culture glitz of mainstreamed media productions, under the American nightmare of individualistic ambition, there is something real, something that lasts, something our truest hearts long for. We just need to excavate it.

As Latina mothers entering the second phase of adulthood, we can take the traits and habits built by mothering—patience, maturity, kindness, empathy, resourcefulness, long-term planning, delayed gratification—and turn them toward meaningful social, artistic, professional, and political endeavors. Our beautiful, broken world needs all the help it can get, and the public sphere cries out for the skills and sensitivities inculcated in us by the experience of motherhood. But at the same time, we can resist commitments—whether to people or to institutions—that are all-consuming in the way that motherhood can be. We can choose to save time and energy for ourselves.

It's true that some wiser mothers, younger mothers—women from the middle and upper classes, women raised to have self-esteem, women who delayed childbearing and childrearing until later in life—may have managed to find all this out before their mothering experience began. They may have structured their lives so as to preserve time, energy, and attention for themselves even while raising their children. *Respeto*. More power to them. But many Latinas of my generation, pressured by cultural norms of *familia* and *marianismo* and still often constrained by financial lack, continue to give birth at earlier ages than do upper- and middle-class Anglo women. Many of us continue to configure our identities around our children, and as we become significant, primary, or sole breadwinners for our families, our careers become an additional priority we may enjoy but are also quick to justify with the claim that our labor ensures our children's well-being. Despite the gains of Xicanisma and Latinas' entry into the professions, many of us here on the ground continue to prioritize family above self, our children's development above our own. Numerous cultural and economic forces conspire against the unfolding and creating of our identities.

So if it takes us until later in life to learn to foreground ourselves: well, better late than never. Shaped by cultural identity and the experience of maternal alterity, we remain permanently out of step with mainstream white cultural images of women our age. This difference offers us resistant ground on which to stand.

As I'm writing this by hand on a sunny Saturday morning, sitting on our sofa, my foot against the hip of my husband, who's reading the *New York Times* and crunching his toast, I can look across the room to the bright watercolor painting of my grandparents' house flanked by palm trees in Key West, the house where my father, aunts, and uncle grew up. Sometimes I long to go back there, to that old, comfortable configuration of *familia*, of warmth and love and food.

But my father has been gone for years now, my mother hasn't spoken to me since *The Truth Book* appeared, and my brother lives with his family in Texas. Our family's home in Key West was sold long ago to wealthy Miami decorators who turned it into a pricey bed-and-breakfast. Key West, its population half Cuban in the 1890s, when my great-grandparents ran the Spanish print shop and printed the island's Spanish newspaper, is now too prohibitively expensive for most of us. My only relative who still dwells in Cayo Hueso is my divorced aunt Lourdes, who waited until her children were through high school before pursuing her own education. Now a librarian at Key West High, she's holding out until retirement, when she'll move north to Gainesville to live near her two sisters. These three sisters, my aunts, will spend their next phase of life in each other's company. When they were young in the 1950s and '60s, full of dreams of marriage and children, it's perhaps not what they would have imagined for themselves: an old age of sisterhood. Yet they are happy, excited, content.

There is no way back. We can only dream our way forward, creating new affiliations. I'm moving from an old identity constructed by the sacrifices of mothering into a paradigm of mutual sistering: older sisters, younger sisters, sisters across a spectrum of age and experience, varied peers that leave room for the self to flourish. *Mis hermanas, mis comadres, mil gracias.* I can't yet say what it will mean. I thought I was grown up, but I'm still changing. I can feel it, chart it, but I don't yet know how it will end.

At the climax of the stage version of *Real Women Have Curves*, all five Chicanas undress down to their underwear and embrace: the mother, her daughters, and their two coworkers, ranging in age from eighteen to forty-eight. "*They all hug in a semicircle laughing triumphantly,*" read the stage directions.

Mutual laughter reconfigures their futures, paves the way forward. The boundaries that divide them soften. Rigid roles melt away. Their embrace is a transformative moment of collective sensuality, joy, and self-acceptance that lays the groundwork for their economic solidarity and the achievement of their creative and professional dreams. Older and younger, experienced and naive, they hold each other and love themselves, and they are changed.

"We can finally relax," rejoices Ana, the eighteen-year-old.

But her older, wiser sister Estela replies, "We're not finished yet."

GRATITUDE

To Kristen Elias Rowley, humanities editor at the University of Nebraska Press, who believed in this collection from the beginning.

To Norma Cantú and Sandra Cisneros, first readers, for the many helpful suggestions that improved these essays and for the inspiration of their own lives and work.

To my agent, Mitchell Waters, for his unstinting faith in my voice and his generous help.

To Lorraine López, without whose kind invitations two of these essays would not exist, for her friendship.

To all of the editors who've invited, accepted, and strengthened these pieces over the years.

To my graduate research assistant Sinduja Sathiyaseelan, for her thoughtful and meticulous help with this manuscript, and to the Department of English at the University of Nebraska–Lincoln, for providing me with such an able assistant.

To all our new friends in Nebraska, for welcoming us here, and to all our old friends far away. We miss you.

To my magical, wondrous family, with love.

SOURCE ACKNOWLEDGMENTS

The following essays appeared in different form in the following publications:

"Island of Bones," *The Other Latino: Writing against a Singular Identity*, ed. Blas Falconer and Lorraine M. Lopez. © 2011 by The Arizona Board of Regents. Reprinted by permission of the University of Arizona Press.

"What My Mother Told Me When I Found Her," *Hip Mama* 33 (2005), and *The Truth Book*, 1–2 (Arcade, 2005). Reprinted by permission of Skyhorse Publishing.

"Clips of My Father's House," *Wabash Magazine* (Winter/Spring 2001): 28–30, and *Key West: A Collection*, ed. Brett Van Emst (White Fish Press, 2001), and *The Truth Book*, 54–57 (Arcade, 2005). Reprinted by permission of Skyhorse Publishing.

"Turn of Faith," *The New York Times Magazine*, August 14, 2005. © 2005 by Joy Castro.

"In Theory," *Quarterly West* 40 (1995): 39–41. © 1995 by Joy Castro.

"Farm Use," *Without a Net: The Female Experience of Growing Up Working*

Class, ed. Michelle Tea, 21–28 (Seal Press, 2004), and *The Truth Book*, 73, 97–99, 104, 118–19, 121–23, 149–52 (Arcade, 2005). Reprinted by permission of Skyhorse Publishing.

"Hip Joints," *Indiana Review* 32, no. 2 (2010): 117–24. © 2010 by Joy Castro.

"Edging," *Mid-American Review* 12, no. 1 (1991): 67–69, and *Breeder: Real-Life Stories from the New Generation of Mothers*, ed. Ariel Gore and Bee Lavender, 150–53 (Seal Press, 2001). © 1991 by Joy Castro.

"The Athens of the Midwest," *Cream City Review* 27, no. 2 (2003): 21–28. © 2003 by Joy Castro.

"An Angle of Vision," *An Angle of Vision: Women Writers on Their Poor and Working-Class Roots*, ed. Lorraine M. López (University of Michigan Press, 2009), 184–92. © 2009 by Joy Castro.

"On Becoming Educated," *The Scholar and Feminist Online* 8, no. 3 (2010) (published by The Barnard Center for Research on Women). © 2010 by Joy Castro.

"Grip," *Fourth Genre: Explorations in Nonfiction* 11, no. 2 (2009): 119–20, and *Quavering between Song and Story: Essays for the Twenty-First Century*, ed. Sheryl St. Germain and Margaret Whitford (Autumn House Press, 2010), 45–46. © 2009 by Joy Castro.

"Getting 'Grip,'" *Fourth Genre: Explorations in Nonfiction* 11, no. 2 (2009): 121–27. © 2009 by Joy Castro.

"Vesper Adest," *Seneca Review* 39, no. 2 & 40, no. 1 (2010): 136–38. © 2010 by Joy Castro.

NOTES

ISLAND OF BONES

1 *"first* wave of Cubans": Grenier, "Creation and Maintenance," 212.

GETTING LOST

21 "Only a house quiet as snow": Cisneros, *House on Mango Street,* 108.

FITTING

56 "Women have served": Woolf, *Room of One's Own,* 35.
57 "the best of husbands": Woolf, *Room of One's Own,* 60.

AN ANGLE OF VISION

71 When at seventeen I dropped out: According to Paul Tough, "What It Takes to Make a Student," children in professional homes, by the age of three, have heard an average of 500,000 encouragements, "words of praise and approval," and only 80,000 discouragements, "prohibitions and words of disapproval," a ratio of more than six to one, whereas in the kind of home where my brother and I grew up, the situation is reversed. Children are spoken to 305,000 fewer times overall, and the utterances they hear have a ratio of 2.5 discouragements to 1 encouragement (48). We grew up in a house of *no's,* a

house where questions would get you a slap or a *Watch your mouth*. "In public life," Tough explains, "the qualities that middle-class children develop are consistently valued over the ones that poor and working-class children develop. Middle-class children," since they are talked to and encouraged by adults, "become used to adults taking their concerns seriously, and so they grow up with a sense of entitlement, which gives them a confidence, in the classroom and elsewhere, that less-wealthy children lack." They feel comfortable testing ideas verbally in a group; they feel comfortable spending time and energy on things (like seminar discussions) with no immediate practical benefit. They have "an array of advantages," while "the manner in which [poor children] are raised puts them at a disadvantage in the measures that count in contemporary American society." While the lack of material goods—books, food, museum visits—certainly has an effect, Tough posits that "the real advantages that middle-class children gain come from more elusive processes: the language that their parents use, the attitudes toward life that they convey" (49).

71 **"You save yourself":** Sebold, *Lucky*, 61.

72 **In the Europe of the 1200s:** Danziger and Gillingham, *1215*, 3.

74 **"authorize [my] desire":** Pérez, *Decolonial Imaginary*, 102.

VESPER ADEST

102 **Title:** Catullus, *Poems of Catullus*, 122. "Vesper adest" are the opening words of poem 62, an epithalamium, or wedding poem, by Catullus, a Roman poet of the first century BC. They mean "Evening is come," and they refer to a specific moment of celebration: the moment when the bride and groom leave the feast to retire alone together for the first time. It is a song of consummation.

"¿QUIÉN ES ESE JIMMY CHOO?"

110 **Looking ahead to a future:** Three years ago, when I first wondered these things, I couldn't have anticipated the global economic crisis we now face. The conundrum of disposable income may, after our son graduates next year, be forced off my plate by circumstance. In a moment when lawyers in their forties are forced to move back home with their parents, he might, like many young people, be unable to

find paid work; my mothering may continue in new forms. Even if he manages to achieve economic independence, my husband and I may struggle, our anticipated financial margin evaporating in the fluctuating economy as our retirement funds already have. Stewarding my disposable income may be something I won't need to worry about.

But three years ago, I didn't know that.

112 **Anzaldúa uses a birth metaphor:** Anzaldúa, *Interviews*, 225–26. Women who have experienced actual childbirth, I have noticed, rarely use birth as a metaphor for anything else. For us, birth is too physically and psychically overwhelming, too wholly transformative, to be employed for anything smaller. We know it to be irreducible.

Yet I am sympathetic to Anzaldúa's use of birth imagery here, because I think she resorts to it due to the dearth of terms our culture offers to describe the evolution or metamorphosis of identity. This deep change in the self is so dark and quiet and fumbling a process: inchoate, inarticulate. We don't have words to talk about it or social spaces in which we're invited to discuss it, and we rarely hear our elders describe their own such processes. It is more private, in some ways, than sex.

112 *In the middle of the road*: There are many translations of these famous first lines from *The Divine Comedy*. This is my own amalgamation.

114 **"Not a man's house":** Cisneros, *House on Mango Street*, 108.

119 **But many Latinas of my generation:** Coined by Elsa Chaney and popularized by Evelyn Stevens in her 1973 article "Marianismo," the concept of *marianismo* has been widely criticized by Latinas on various counts, including that of being a North American conceptual imposition upon Latin American women's femininity practices and ideologies, which have been mischaracterized by U.S. Anglo feminists as excessively passive. Nonetheless, I use it here because some Latinas still see the concept as speaking to an important element of the belief system with which we were raised. However imperfect the term, I employ it in a kind of shorthand to acknowledge the feminine ideal that was impressed upon many of us: sexual and moral purity, self-sacrifice, modesty, spiritual strength, and the centrality of children in one's life.

121 *"They all hug in a semicircle"*: López, *Real Women Have Curves*, 286.

BIBLIOGRAPHY

Anzaldúa, Gloria. *Borderlands/La Frontera: The New Mestiza*. San Francisco: Aunt Lute Books, 1987.

———. *Interviews: Entrevistas*. New York: Routledge, 2000.

Catullus, Gaius Valerius. *The Poems of Catullus: A Bilingual Edition*. Trans. Peter Green. Berkeley: University of California Press, 2005.

Cisneros, Sandra. *The House on Mango Street*. 1984. New York: Vintage, 1991.

Danziger, Danny, and John Gillingham. *1215: The Year of Magna Carta*. 2003. New York: Touchstone, 2005.

Greenblatt, Stephen. "Meet the Writers: Stephen Greenblatt." Interview. Barnes and Noble, 2004. Available at http://www.barnesandnoble .com/writers/writerdetails.asp?userid=AG6YcY2DW0&cid=1305369 #interview.

Grenier, Guillermo J. "The Creation and Maintenance of the Cuban American 'Exile Ideology': Evidence from the FIU Cuba Poll 2004." *Journal of American Ethnic History* 25 (2006): 209–24.

hooks, bell. "Eating the Other: Desire and Resistance." In *Eating Culture*, ed. Ron Scapp and Brian Seltz, 181–200. Albany: SUNY Press, 1998.

———. "Out of the Academy and Into the Streets." *Ms. Magazine* 3, no. 1 (1992): 80–82.

López, Josefina. *Real Women Have Curves*. In *Latino Boom: An Anthology of U.S. Latino Literature*, ed. John S. Christie and José B. Gonzalez, 254–99. New York: Pearson Longman, 2006.

Pérez, Emma. *The Decolonial Imaginary: Writing Chicanas into History*. Bloomington: Indiana University Press, 1999.

Rumi, Jelaluddin. *Open Secret: Versions of Rumi*. Trans. John Moyne and Coleman Barks. Putney VT: Threshold, 1984.

Sebold, Alice. *Lucky*. 1999. New York: Little, Brown, 2002.

Slepoy, Graciela Susana Moreira. "An Exploration of Gloria Anzaldúa's Feminist Thought in *Borderlands/La Frontera: The New Mestiza*." Proceedings, 2003 Hawaii International Conference on Arts and Humanities. Available at http://www.hichumanities.org/AHproceedings/.

Stevens, Evelyn P. "Marianismo: The Other Side of Machismo in Latin America." In *Female and Male in Latin America: Essays*, ed. Ann Pescatello, 90–101. Pittsburgh: University of Pittsburgh Press, 1973.

Tough, Paul. "What It Takes to Make a Student." *New York Times Magazine*, 26 November 2006, 44–51, 69–72, 77.

Woolf, Virginia. *A Room of One's Own*. 1929. New York: Harcourt, 2005.

IN THE AMERICAN LIVES SERIES

Fault Line
by Laurie Alberts

Pieces from Life's Crazy Quilt
by Marvin V. Arnett

Songs from the Black Chair:
A Memoir of Mental Illness
by Charles Barber

This Is Not the Ivy League:
A Memoir
by Mary Clearman Blew

Driving with Dvořák: Essays on
Memory and Identity
by Fleda Brown

Searching for Tamsen Donner
by Gabrielle Burton

Island of Bones: Essays
by Joy Castro

American Lives: A Reader
edited by Alicia Christensen
introduced by Tobias Wolff

Out of Joint: A Private and Public
Story of Arthritis
by Mary Felstiner

Descanso for My Father:
Fragments of a Life
by Harrison Candelaria Fletcher

Falling Room
by Eli Hastings

Opa Nobody
by Sonya Huber

Hannah and the Mountain: Notes
toward a Wilderness Fatherhood
by Jonathan Johnson

Local Wonders: Seasons in the
Bohemian Alps
by Ted Kooser

Bigger than Life: A Murder,
a Memoir
by Dinah Lenney

What Becomes You
by Aaron Raz Link and Hilda Raz

Such a Life
by Lee Martin

Turning Bones
by Lee Martin

In Rooms of Memory: Essays
by Hilary Masters

Between Panic and Desire
by Dinty W. Moore

Sleep in Me
by Jon Pineda

Thoughts from a Queen-Sized Bed
by Mimi Schwartz

*My Ruby Slippers: Finding Place
on the Road Back to Kansas*
by Tracy Seeley

The Fortune Teller's Kiss
by Brenda Serotte

*Gang of One: Memoirs of a Red
Guard*
by Fan Shen

Just Breathe Normally
by Peggy Shumaker

Scraping By in the Big Eighties
by Natalia Rachel Singer

In the Shadow of Memory
by Floyd Skloot

*Secret Frequencies: A New York
Education*
by John Skoyles

Phantom Limb
by Janet Sternburg

*Yellowstone Autumn: A Season of
Discovery in a Wondrous Land*
by W. D. Wetherell

To order or obtain more
information on these or other
University of Nebraska Press titles,
visit www.nebraskapress.unl.edu.